Prosperity
KILLERS

JOEL
SIEGEL

CONTENTS

The blessing of the Lord makes rich,

and he adds no sorrow with it.

Proverbs 10:22

INTRODUCTION

I was privileged to travel for seven years with Rev. Kenneth E. Hagin as part of his crusade team. During those years, I sat on the front row in his services, listening intently as he imparted wisdom from his more than seventy years of ministry. I followed his ministry closely, and continue to do so today.

One of the many outstanding characteristics about Brother Hagin's ministry was the way that he dealt with the subject of money and finances. Brother Hagin saw many other ministers come and go during his years of ministry; many were his contemporaries from earlier years who had dropped off the scene. The reason for their downfall? An improper emphasis on money. Abuses were rampant in his day, and Brother Hagin credited these abuses with causing the great healing revival of the 1950's to dissipate.

Brother Hagin had several visitations from the Lord over the years, which brought revelation and instruction in many areas, including the area of finances. There were two things in particular that the Lord told him that have stuck with me throughout the years; I heard him mention these things over and over during my time on the road with him. The first thing he would talk about is something the Lord said to him in a vision in 1950. These were Jesus' words:

Be very careful about money. Many, upon whom I have placed my anointing, have become money-minded and have lost the anointing.

Jesus was no doubt referring, in part, to the many healing evangelists who were improperly emphasizing finances. They had indeed become money-minded, lost the anointing, and had fallen from their place of prominence in ministry. By making this statement, Jesus reinforced a central teaching of Scripture: money is no small issue, rather, it is a great responsibility. How we view and handle money can make us or break us, even affecting our spiritual life.

Brother Hagin heeded these words of Jesus, conducting more than seven decades of ministry without financial misstep, scandal, or fraud. His family, since his death, has continued to run his ministry honorably. I like following after people who have that kind of track record.

The second story that Brother Hagin often shared had to do with an encounter he had with the Lord in 1959. Jesus again appeared to him and, during the course of the vision, spoke to him about money. This is what He said:

If you will learn to follow My Spirit, I will make you rich. I am not opposed to my children being rich; I am only opposed to their being covetous.

How enlightening this statement must have been for Brother Hagin. What a blessing it is for us. The prevailing view in Brother Hagin's day was that the Lord *was* opposed to His children being rich. These words of Jesus (in complete agreement with Scripture) would have indeed been a shock to many. I was blessed to have heard Brother Hagin recount these two visitations many times over the years.

These two words of instruction from Jesus represent two sides of what remains a very misunderstood and controversial truth: the subject of prosperity. We must embrace both sides of this truth: the side of caution and the side of blessing. We err if we *only* talk about being rich, never heeding any of the Bible's other words about money. And, we err if we are cautious to the point of never receiving *the blessing of the Lord that makes rich* (Proverbs 10:22).

There are ditches of error – extremes – on both sides of the road to blessing. On the one side, we cannot become money-minded, trading the full truth of God's Word for a one-sided, self-absorbed, all-about-me gospel. Like it or not, a certain amount of suffering and self-denial are part of the Christian life. The ditch on the other side of the road, however, may be the more common one: failing to recognize and embrace the fullness of our redemption. We must constantly proclaim the blessed truth that God wants us fully supplied, and will abundantly provide.

The fastest path to prosperity is found by traveling down the middle of the road, avoiding the ditches of error on either side. The middle of the road is a place of balance, where all different sides of the truth are embraced. Brother Hagin successfully fulfilled seven decades of ministry by remaining balanced. Balance often eludes the Body of Christ, as we tend to gravitate to one side of the road or the other. This book seeks to bring balance to the subject of prosperity: a subject victimized by extremes.

Many tests will confront the believer where prosperity is concerned. We must consecrate ourselves sufficiently to God, passing those tests. Those who pass God's tests will enjoy God's best. Those who fail God's tests will eventually disqualify themselves from God's best. Some of these areas of disqualification are common; I call them *prosperity killers*. A primary purpose of this book is to help us identify and avoid these prosperity killers.

The tasks assigned us by God in the last days require large sums and vast resources. The plan of God is serious business. The time left until Jesus returns is short, and God's harvest is great. We must have the necessary funds available to accomplish His work. Prosperity is not an option; we must not succumb to the prosperity killers.

Chapter 1

HELP ON THE ROAD

Everyone wants prosperity.

The term *prosperity* simply means *to succeed*. No one sets out on a venture wishing for failure; all desire success. We want things to go well with us (that's another definition of prosperity: *to have it go well*). We want it to go well with our business, with the economy, with our friends, and with our family. We so desire prosperity for our children that we will sacrifice to make sure they have every possible advantage in life. No parent wants their child to have any less than they had. Only the best for our kids.

God is no different. His desire for the well being of His children is intense, exceeding the desires we have for our kids. He wants us to succeed more than we want to succeed. This verse below, penned by the Apostle John, is a picture of the Father's desire for all His children. It's His will for you.

*Beloved, I pray that **all may go well with you** and that you may be in good health, as it goes well with your soul.*

3 John 1:2

The New King James Version of the Bible says it this way:

*Beloved, I pray that **you may prosper in all things** and be in health, just as your soul prospers.*

The Greek word translated here as *prosper* literally means *help on the road*. As one who travels and spends time on the road, I appreciate that definition. The phrase *on the road* indicates a journey: a starting point and a finish line. If life is anything, it is a series of journeys. We find ourselves constantly on the move, always in motion. Thank God, we have help on life's road. We need not attempt these journeys on our own.

Prosperity means that we always arrive safely, successfully completing each of life's journeys. Every endeavor that we undertake flourishes, every project succeeds. Our continued success is not only due to our own efforts and strength, but also due to the help that is offered us from God. We must accept His help, avoiding the kind of ugly, proud attitude that insists on doing everything ourselves. Many insist on pulling themselves up by their own bootstraps: becoming a self-made man. Most self-made men I know are a mess. There is no true prosperity without the help that comes from God.

The help that God offers us is supernatural, allowing us to accomplish what our humanity alone could not. With His help, we can do what we otherwise could not, have what we otherwise could not, give what we otherwise could not, and enjoy what we otherwise would not.

*Give us this day our **daily bread**.*

Matthew 6:11

God, our Provider, wants us to learn to look to Him daily. He's an everyday God, not just a once-a-week (or one Sunday a month) God. He wants to be constantly involved in our lives. Of course, there is effort required on our part as well. God can't prosper us without us. It's *help on the road*, not *help on the couch* while we sit around, doing nothing. We must have our feet on the ground, our hand to the plow. To enjoy God's prosperity is to put forth effort, naturally and spiritually, working with Him to receive His best. We have His help on the road only if we are on the road – following His path – looking to Him daily for His provision.

Chapter 2

RICH

God is interested in our prosperity; He wants it to be well with us.

That's a nice thought, but for many, that's all it is: just a nice thought. People hear these things and go on their way without recognizing the magnitude of what they heard. There's so much more to this subject, however, than just nice thoughts and well-wishes. Prosperity is not an *Oh, by-the-way* topic that we mention once a year just to say we preached on it. This truth – God's desire for our well being – is at the very heart of the gospel. It's so central to the plan of God that when Jesus introduced His ministry to the people in His hometown, He read a passage from Isaiah that began with prosperity.

*The Spirit of the Lord is upon me, because he has anointed me to proclaim **good news to the poor**. He has sent me to proclaim liberty to the captives and recovering of sight to the blind, to set at liberty those who are oppressed.*

Luke 4:18

Was this just a slip of the tongue or a one-time honorable mention? No. Three chapters later, Jesus again summarizes His ministry, again including prosperity.

And he answered them, Go and tell John what you have seen and heard: the blind receive their sight, the lame walk, lepers *are cleansed, and the deaf hear, the dead are raised up, **the poor have good news preached to them**.*

Luke 7:22

This is outstanding. Look at the company in which prosperity finds itself: blind people seeing, crippled people walking, incurable leprosy vanishing, deaf people hearing, and the dead rising again to life. Is good news to the poor really worthy of mention among the works of might in this passage? Many would think not, however, Jesus included it, not randomly but purposely. He lets us know that prosperity is by no means an afterthought. It's right in the thick of the most amazing works of God.

Notice that this verse didn't say the poor received handouts, food vouchers, or housing assistance. (It's scriptural, of course, to minister to the poor in tangible ways, but we must understand that temporal assistance is never the permanent answer for poverty.) The poor received the gospel: good news. The gospel is the answer for the poor person, not handouts. Poverty is not eradicated by getting something, it's eradicated by knowing something. The good news – knowledge of how to function in the Kingdom of God – will bring anyone out of poverty. Good news to the poor is as precious and significant as sight to the blind or life to the dead.

The gospel that Jesus preached included deliverance from poverty. It had to. Can you imagine Jesus, after opening the ears of the deaf and the eyes of the blind, turning to the poor, saying, *Now, I know it's tough for you guys down here, but I have good news for you: you'll get to Heaven someday where it's not so bad?*

No! The poor person who heard Jesus preach learned that their poverty faced the same fate as leprosy, blindness, deafness, and premature death. It was abolished; annihilated. The gospel of Jesus is not just a guarantee of Heaven; it encompasses our entire life, earthly and heavenly.

MADE RICH

For you know the grace of our Lord Jesus Christ, that though he was rich, yet for your sake he became poor, so that you by his poverty might become rich.

2 Corinthians 8:9

The person who approaches God's Word intellectually (rather than receiving by simple faith) would filter this verse through theological thought or religious tradition, forcing it to say something other than what it really says. I've heard such people explain that this verse is really talking about spiritual riches, not material riches.

Is it possible to be spiritually rich? Certainly. It's actually a requirement for the believer. Paul, speaking to the church at Colossae, encouraged them to allow the Word to *dwell in them richly* (Colossians 3:16). We already read 3 John 1:2, which says we will prosper *as our soul prospers.* So yes, we are to be spiritually rich. Being rich in spirit is not what this verse is talking about at all, however. 2 Corinthians chapters eight and nine are speaking exclusively of material riches: cold, hard cash. The word *rich* in this verse refers to money – financial and material wealth – nothing else.

JESUS: POOR AND RICH

. . . . though he was rich, yet for your sake he became poor, so that you by his poverty might become rich.

2 Corinthians 8:9

We must answer these important questions: When was Jesus rich, and when did He become poor?

Jesus was a partaker of God's riches in glory from eternity past. He was also rich upon the earth. Not long after He arrived as a baby, extravagant monetary gifts from unlikely sources showed up, sustaining He and His family. Those who say Jesus lived in poverty because He was born in a barn are forgetting this part of the story.

Much of what we know about Jesus' life on Earth is found in the gospels. Contrary to religious belief, the gospels just don't depict a man who was poor. Quite the opposite. He always had plenty of the best of everything He needed. The one time that we see Jesus experiencing lack, He dealt with it immediately and severely.

On the following day, when they came from Bethany, he was hungry. And seeing in the distance a fig tree in leaf, he went to see if he could find anything on it. When he came to it, he found nothing but leaves, for it was not the season for figs. And he said to it, "May no one ever eat fruit from you again." And his disciples heard it.

Mark 11:12-14

This tree, being in leaf, advertised provision but instead surprised Jesus with lack. Jesus didn't adapt to lack when it showed up in His life. Instead, He rebuked it and forbade it. He took a hardline stance against poverty, denying it any place in Him. Full provision was what He expected as He performed the will of God, nothing less. Full provision – a full supply – is what the Bible means when it uses the word *rich*.

Jesus simply was not poor on the earth. When He needed a ride into town, the brand new colt, *upon which no man had ever sat*, was there waiting for Him (Luke 19:30). When He needed a banquet facility for the Passover meal, a large, furnished upper room – the penthouse suite – was ready and waiting. Wealthy women regularly donated to His ministry. The robe He wore to His crucifixion was evidently of the highest quality (the Roman soldiers gambled to see who would get it after He had died). In both Heaven and on Earth, Jesus was fully supplied. He was rich.

When, then, did Jesus become poor? He became poor when He became sin: at the cross. When Jesus suffered the curse of sin, He also took upon Himself the curse of poverty. Notice the redemptive language used in the verse we have been studying:

> *For you know the grace of our Lord Jesus Christ, that though he was rich, yet **for your sake he became poor**, so that you by his poverty might become rich.*
>
> *2 Corinthians 8:9*

This verse speaks of Jesus taking something He didn't deserve (our poverty), so that we could have something we didn't deserve (His prosperity). He didn't deserve our poverty, yet He took it upon Himself, becoming poor in our place. We didn't deserve His riches and provision, yet the Master, by His grace, redeemed us unto that very thing. He took our poverty, we got His riches. He was made poor, we were made rich. This great exchange took place way back when Jesus died on the cross.

Any time the Bible speaks of Christ taking something from us in order to give something to us, it's speaking of our redemption: something He died for. Notice how similar this verse sounds to other redemptive verses:

For our sake he made him to be sin who knew no sin, so that in him we might become the righteousness of God.
2 Corinthians 5:21

He was made sin. We were made righteous.

Surely he has borne our griefs (sickness) *and carried our sorrows* (pains); *yet we esteemed him stricken, smitten by God, and afflicted. But he was pierced for our transgressions; he was crushed for our iniquities; upon him was the chastisement that brought us peace, and with his wounds we are healed.*
Isaiah 53:4-5

He took our sicknesses. We received His healing.

For you know the grace of our Lord Jesus Christ, that though he was rich, yet for your sake he became poor, so that you by his poverty might become rich.
2 Corinthians 8:9

He became poor. We were made rich. This is part of our redemption.

Someone may ask, *Wait a second. Are you saying that Jesus died to make us financially rich?* No, I'm not saying that. The Bible says that. I'm just repeating what the Word says. I understand that such statements sound sacrilegious to people. It sounds like we are cheapening His sacrifice by reducing it to money in our pocket. To think those things is perfectly natural, but we are not to think according to the natural. We are to renew our minds to the truth, changing our thinking to match the Word of God.

The truth is, He died to provide. He bore wounds on His back for us to have more than enough. He had spikes driven through His hands so that we could give freely to the work of God. It does not cheapen redemption to boldly declare these things, it honors it. What cheapens His sacrifice is failing to recognize the magnitude of it: applying the great work of redemption to just one area instead of celebrating its all-inclusive greatness.

Israel, put your hope in the Lord, for with the Lord is unfailing love and with him is ***full redemption***.

Psalms 130:7 (NIV)

Our redemption includes deliverance from sin, and everything that came into the earth as a result of sin, namely sickness and poverty. Just as we are no longer slaves to sin, we have been set free from the bondage of poverty. He was made poor so we might be rich.

The majority of the Body of Christ does not believe that divine provision is part of our redemption. They devote none of their faith toward possessing this part of our inheritance. Of those who do believe in prosperity as a Bible doctrine, many consider it a side issue of minor importance: not much more than a pleasant thought or wishful thinking. The Body of Christ must consider this truth more carefully, taking a closer look and seeking the proper perspective.

OUR RESPONSIBILITY

If provision is part of our redemption, then a great price was paid to secure it. The benefits of redemption are free to us, but were obtained at great cost: the precious, sinless blood of Christ. When Jesus shed His blood, it was not an easy, casual event, but the most torturous event imaginable. He suffered without mercy so you and I could enjoy the full redemption that's ours.

Let's talk of this in even more personal terms. He suffered for *your* prosperity. He died to provide for *you*. He was tormented for *me*. Do these things mean anything to us? They don't to the multitudes who dismiss this subject in favor of more non-confrontational topics. If we dismiss this subject, or treat it lightly or casually, then in this area of our lives, Christ's wounds were in vain. His suffering was for nothing as far as we are concerned. Let's never allow this to be the case.

We must adopt thinking that says, *If Christ died for it, I'm responsible for it.* If God loved me so much that He sent Christ to die – not just for my sins, but also for my prosperity – then I have the responsibility to embrace that part of my redemption as much as I embrace my deliverance from sin.

Is financial prosperity the biggest part of the Christian life? Certainly not. All the provision in the world means nothing if a person dies and goes to Hell. But, just because it's not the *most* important thing doesn't make it unimportant. Jesus suffered the curse of poverty so I could live in prosperity and blessing. This is not some self-gratifying, inward-pointing, hedonistic teaching; it's holy, a truth to be revered. Blood was shed so my temporal needs could be met. Our redemption extends to every area of our lives. We must not diminish nor be embarrassed of these truths, rather, we exalt them. He saved us, He healed us, He has made us rich.

Chapter 3
PROSPERITY HATERS

The subject of Bible prosperity is not the brain child of a few money-hungry preachers looking to fleece God's sheep. Nor is it a doctrine based on just a few isolated scriptures. Prosperity is God's idea – part of redemption's plan from before the foundation of the world – a theme woven throughout the entire Bible. Prosperity so abounds in the pages of Scripture that one must turn away from the Word to miss it. Below are some of the verses from just one book of the Bible, the book of Psalms, that speak of God's desire for our well being. I recommend reading these verses slowly, out loud if possible, to receive their full impact. (Excitement warning: you may start praising or shouting while reading these verses.)

He is like a tree planted by streams of water that yields its fruit in its season, and its leaf does not wither. In all that he does, he prospers. Psalms 1:3

He brought me forth also into a large place; He was delivering me because He was pleased with me and delighted in me. Psalms 18:19 (AMP)

THE LORD is my Shepherd [to feed, guide, and shield me], I shall not lack. He makes me lie down in [fresh, tender] green pastures; He leads me beside the still and restful waters. Psalms 23:1-2 (AMP)

You prepare a table before me in the presence of my enemies. You anoint my head with oil; my [brimming] cup runs over. Psalms 23:5 (AMP)

Let those who favor my righteous cause and have pleasure in my uprightness shout for joy and be glad and say continually, Let the Lord be magnified, Who takes pleasure in the prosperity of His servant. Psalms 35:27 (AMP)

Delight yourself in the Lord, and he will give you the desires of your heart. Psalms 37:4

They are not put to shame in evil times; in the days of famine they have abundance. Psalms 37:19

The wicked borrows but does not pay back, but the righteous is generous and gives. Psalms 37:21

I have been young, and now am old, yet I have not seen the righteous forsaken or his children begging for bread. He is ever lending generously, and his children become a blessing. Psalms 37:25-26

You let men ride over our heads; we went through fire and through water; yet you have brought us out to a place of abundance. Psalms 66:12

For the Lord God is a sun and shield; the Lord bestows favor and honor. No good thing does he withhold from those who walk uprightly. Psalms 84:11

He fills my life with good things. My youth is renewed like the eagle's! Psalms 103:5 (NLT)

The Lord brought his people out of Egypt, loaded with silver and gold; and not one among the tribes of Israel even stumbled. Psalms 105:37 (NLT)

Praise the Lord! How joyful are those who fear the Lord and delight in obeying his commands. Their children will be successful everywhere; an entire generation of godly people will be blessed. They themselves will be wealthy, and their good deeds will last forever. Psalms 112:1-3 (NLT)

May the Lord give you increase, you and your children! May you be blessed by the Lord, who made heaven and earth! The heavens are the Lord's heavens, but the earth he has given to the children of man. Psalms 115:14-16

Glory! What great scriptures. Prosperity and increase are everywhere in the Word, not just in Psalms. This truth resonates throughout the pages of the Bible, which makes the fact that the majority of the Body of Christ opposes – even hates – the doctrine of prosperity all the more difficult to understand. It's true, the subject of prosperity is despised and rejected by Christians everywhere.

There are also other Bible subjects from which believers turn away. People have long opposed speaking in tongues, purposing to never embrace that experience. Many also oppose the doctrine of healing, taking offense when someone suggests that healing is God's will. (These same believers, however, pray continually for the healing of themselves and others, doing everything medically possible to stay alive.) People everywhere are opposed to tongues and healing, yet opposition in those areas is mild compared with the utter disdain that people have for the doctrine of prosperity.

Why all the angst? The logic goes something like this: *tongues or healing doesn't really hurt anyone, but prosperity hurts vulnerable people, causing them to see God differently than He really is and robbing them of their hard-earned money.* That might not be a very good reason (since it's not true), but it is a common reason nonetheless.

I simply cannot overstate the level of anger that many Christians have toward the subject of Bible prosperity. I've seen people just about lose it when the subject was mentioned. Respected Christian leaders everywhere describe the message of prosperity as an abomination, a doctrine of devils, wickedness, and even witchcraft. Charismatics and fundamentalists alike find unity in their intense opposition to this subject, writing books and articles, producing radio broadcasts and videos; anything to combat the message of prosperity.

Like those that oppose healing but long to be healed, prosperity opponents work long hours, trying to earn enough money to support their families. They hope for promotions and raises at work, and pray that their retirement and investment accounts flourish. Does this all seem a bit hypocritical? If prosperity is so bad, why are the people who are against it pursuing it? If it's that devilish, why have any of it? Why not just subsist on barely enough to get by? It's wrong to preach against something, yet enjoy it yourself.

The truth, as has already been stated, is that *everyone* wants prosperity. Not everyone, however, believes that God has anything to do with it.

Believers who oppose the message of prosperity – I call them *prosperity haters* – are good, well-meaning, born-again people. The books they write and the messages they preach against prosperity may not be worthy of our attention, but the people themselves are still brothers and sisters in the Lord, worthy of our respect. Many have answered the call of God, are ministering to the best of their ability, and in some cases have won many souls to Jesus. I'm truly not against anyone, but we need to figure out why such division exists in this area.

MOUNTAINS

The reason for the divide lies in this observation from a great preacher long ago: *Bible truths are like the different sides of a mountain. The view looking up one side is somewhat different than the view from the other side, yet it's all the same mountain.* What wisdom. There are different sides, or aspects, to Bible truths. This doesn't mean that we are free to change God's Word, nor are we to just pick the one side of the mountain that we like, ignoring all else. No, we must allow the Word of God to show us the view from all sides, forming a complete picture.

Think, for example, about the subject of love. Jesus perfectly exemplified the love of God, yet that love didn't always act the same way. There were times in Jesus' ministry when love brought tender comfort (as He dealt with the woman who was caught in adultery, for example). At other times, His love was a bit more aggressive, such as when He took a whip and beat the money changers out of the temple. Love was His motivation in both instances, but love manifested differently in each instance. We would be wrong to say that love finds someone to whip each day, and would be just as wrong to say that love endorses adultery. Love acts differently in different situations. We must understand the different aspects of love, taking in the big picture.

Many on each side of the truth are guilty of looking at only one side of the mountain. Prosperity teachers have scriptures they use on their side, and prosperity haters have scriptures they use on theirs. Who's right? The Word of God in it's entirety is right. We must embrace all of the Word of God if we are to discover the truth, not just scriptures that serve to prove our point.

One thing is certain: the Bible, in overwhelming fashion, speaks of God as one who blesses His people, not just in Heaven, but on Earth. The scriptures we read from the book of Psalms (along with hundreds of others that speak of our well being) can't all be wrong. Without question, God wants us to prosper. Having said that, I am convinced that the opponents of prosperity are right about some things. There are some truths on their side of the mountain that we must take an honest look at.

THE BIGGEST PROSPERITY HATER

No one hates prosperity more than the devil. A rich Christian, sold out to God, using his resources to advance the Kingdom, is

Satan's biggest nightmare. We see Satan's attitude toward prosperity in his dealings with Job. Satan actually comes before God, complaining about how blessed Job had become. (Satan is the original whiner and complainer, and is the king of prosperity haters.)

Have you not put a hedge around him and his house and all that he has, on every side? You have blessed the work of his hands, and his possessions have increased in the land.

Job 1:10

Notice something very important here (if you're a prosperity hater, read this next statement very carefully): it wasn't Satan who blessed Job, it was God. It wasn't God who afflicted Job, it was Satan. The scriptures state this clearly, in an easy-to-understand manner, but for some reason prosperity haters get it backward. They believe that money and blessings are from the devil, and afflictions are from God.

Satan is the biggest prosperity hater of all. He's also a prosperity stealer, who will try to interfere with the flow of the blessing of the Lord in our lives. Look at this great verse that clearly puts God and the devil on their respective sides of this issue:

The thief comes only to steal and kill and destroy. I came that they may have life and have it abundantly.

John 10:10

God is a good God. Satan is a bad devil. He's the thief, not God. God has never stolen from anyone. Jesus came to give us a high-quality level of life; the same life of abundance that He enjoys. Satan, on the other hand, schemes and plots to steal that abundance. When he steals from someone, the first thing he will say is, *God did this*. Pay no attention to him; he's a known liar. Don't mix up God's role and Satan's role; they never switch places. God is trying to bless you. Satan is trying to steal from you.

I would hate to be aligned with Satan as a prosperity hater here on Earth. Stay off of the devil's side and get over on God's side. The devil works hard to cast doubt in the mind of the believer regarding God's will in this area. He will cause as many delays as possible in hopes that the believer will give up and quit. Never quit your stand of faith. If we quit, Satan wins. If we hold fast, Satan never wins.

Whether we're speaking of lost people, believers, or the devil, you and I are surrounded by prosperity haters. Don't let that bother you. As the urban saying goes: *haters gonna hate*. I'm a believer. Believers gonna believe. Be a prosperity believer, not a prosperity hater.

Chapter 4
PROSPERITY KILLERS

Prosperity belongs to us. It's part of our redemption, a central part of the gospel. The scriptures are replete with verses upon which one can build a solid doctrinal foundation. From God's standpoint, prosperity is a settled fact. Since all this is so, a big question remains: Why do so many of God's people struggle financially? Why are so many experiencing poverty rather than prosperity? Why are so many Christians broke?

It seems as though Bible-believing Christians are one of the poorer people groups in our country. This is even true among churches that preach faith, healing, and prosperity. Prosperity haters have long observed this irony, using it as evidence to fuel their criticisms. They visit large faith churches, observing that the ones who seem to have the most prosperity are the pastors. They conclude that the pastor is preaching prosperity for his own personal financial gain. They assume that he is crooked, preying on the poor people of his congregation.

RICH PREACHERS

I know that some preachers have obtained money by questionable means, violating Paul's instructions in 1 Timothy 3. However, we are not to assume that this is the case all the time, or even the majority of the time. I wonder if it has ever occurred to anyone that the reason why the preacher is blessed might just be that he is actually doing the Word that he preaches? Just a thought.

I have preached prosperity for years. I preached it when I owned no home, living with my Father-in-law, and I preached it when I owned multiple homes at once. The Word that we preach is the same, regardless of circumstance. I have experienced increase over the years and can tell you exactly how it happened: I believed the Word that I was preaching and acted upon it. At no time did my increase come from dropping hints, twisting arms, or asking for even one dollar from the people in my church. God has many avenues through which He can bless His people, and He is able to get provision to us honestly and legally.

The reason why the Church is so broke has nothing to do with God. It's not His will, in fact, it grieves Him. Believers fail to prosper for the same reason they remain chronically ill, or in bondage to sin year after year: they violate the principles of the Word of God and think they will somehow prosper anyway. Simply put, people don't prosper because they don't do the Word.

> *But the one who looks into the perfect law, the law of liberty, and perseveres, being no hearer who forgets but a doer who acts, **he will be blessed in his doing.***
>
> *James 1:25*

MANY KEYS

How does one act upon the Word where prosperity is concerned? Ask that question to ten different people and you may get ten different answers, all of them correct to a degree. Many have learned what they consider to be a key to prosperity, but we must understand that knowing one key is not enough. One key is not the only key.

Take, as an example, the subject of confession. We are correct to emphasize right speaking where money is concerned, but positive confession is just one key among many. Your mouth alone won't get the job done. Other keys, such as faith and prayer, also exist. All these are necessary components of prosperity, but no one thing by itself is the whole enchilada, as they say. A variety of factors, all working together, contribute to one's prosperity.

Since a variety of factors contribute to prosperity, a variety of factors can disqualify a person from prosperity. This is an important truth that all must understand. Here's a sobering thought: a person need not disqualify in every area to ruin their prosperity, they need only miss it in one area.

That's not fair! someone may exclaim. Sure it is. It's how a lot of things work. I don't need every part of my body to fail to end up in bed, I just need one part to not work correctly. I don't need to rob everyone to go to jail, I just need to violate one person. I don't need the entire engine in my car to blow up, just one loose wire will do. This is a lesson I learned just recently.

I had a television mounted on a wall that I needed to take down, so I asked my son to help me. I thought I had disconnected all the wires, but one coaxial cable was still connected as we pulled the set away. The coaxial input on the TV came right out and dangled from the wall, still attached to the cable.

This didn't seem like a big deal. Other than that one input, the TV still worked fine. I ordered the broken part and waited for it to arrive. When it came, I removed about thirty screws from the back of the TV and went to work. One tiny little piece inside was in my way, but I wrestled it out, finished my installation, and put that piece back in place. I don't know what that tiny little piece was, but pulling it out killed the entire television. I had my son help me once more, this time walking the TV out to the curb for the garbage man to take. One little part killed the whole thing.

As I've ministered throughout the years, I've watched many people fall prey to what I call *prosperity killers*. These prosperity killers – areas of disqualification – are easily identified in the Word and are the enemy of the believer. Any one of them can cause a big headache in the believer's life. Several of them together can cause financial ruin. We will spend the remainder of this book learning how to avoid these prosperity killers.

There's a devil who is opposed to your prosperity – a thief who will hinder and delay – but the devil can't kill your prosperity. There are people, saved and unsaved, who oppose prosperity, but other people can't kill your prosperity. Prosperity haters are all around us, but prosperity killers are within us. *Only you can kill your prosperity.* Thank God none of us has to.

Chapter 5

COVETOUSNESS

If then you have been raised with Christ, seek the things that are above, where Christ is, seated at the right hand of God. Set your minds on things that are above, not on things that are on earth. For you have died, and your life is hidden with Christ in God. When Christ who is your life appears, then you also will appear with him in glory. Put to death therefore what is earthly in you: sexual immorality, impurity, passion, evil desire, and covetousness, which is idolatry.

Colossians 3:1-5

Christians tend to believe that since they are saved, covetousness is no longer a problem. Paul, however, understood that covetousness is part of the nature of the flesh which all must continually seek to suppress. Everyone has flesh, and everyone's flesh will covet, if allowed. Paul told us to *crucify our flesh with its passions and desires* (Galatians 5:24).

John, in his writings, also speaks of the desires of the flesh:

Do not love the world or the things in the world. If anyone loves the world, the love of the Father is not in him. For all that is in the world—the desires of the flesh and the desires of the eyes and pride of life—is not from the Father but is from the world.

1 John 2:15-16

As long as we are in this world, we will have to deal with our attraction to the things in the world. Things in this world pull on a person, crying, *Follow me, follow me.* Our job instead is to follow Christ, keeping the things of this world in their place.

How interesting that Paul, in our text in Colossians, listed covetousness right alongside sexual immorality and impurity. Most believers would agree that sleeping around and engaging in sexual perversion is sinful. Not many, however, would place covetousness in that same category. Evidently, to covet is a serious issue with God. Notice that this passage equates covetousness with idolatry. It didn't say that covetousness is *similar* to idolatry, it said it *is* idolatry. Let's define these things:

Giving other things or other people too great a place in your life is idolatry. When you don't yet have those things and you give them a wrong place, it's covetousness.

One need not worship a wall full of statues to be in idolatry. They need only to have priorities that are out of order. Very few believers that I've met bow down and worship false gods, but many, often without realizing it, worship other things. They put *things* ahead of God. These familiar verses, one from the Old Testament and one from the New, speak to this issue, leaving no room for confusion:

You shall have no other gods before me. Exodus 20:3

But seek first the kingdom of God and his righteousness, and all these things will be added to you.

Matthew 6:33

God first. Nothing before Him. We would all like to think that's the picture of our life, but in reality, most people put plenty of other things before God. That's why they struggle so. If seeking God first causes provision and supply to be added to one's life, then failing to seek Him first means provision won't be added; the person's life will suffer loss. Covetousness – putting things and people before God – is a prosperity killer.

Do you give the Word of God five minutes a day, but spend five hours a day consuming media on the internet? If so, there needs to be a dramatic adjusting of priorities. Do you have sports scores and statistics memorized for every team in the league but struggle to think of a single Bible verse to apply to your situation? Priorities. Are you obsessed with clothes, furniture, cars, trucks, motorcycles, boats, or firearms? Things need to change. You may know many other people who are just like you, but you're a Christian. You must be different if you desire the prosperity of God.

Don't misunderstand me. It's okay to enjoy things. It's even okay to enjoy nice things. However, we must not neglect to look at the other side of the mountain. There are multitudes of prosperity-confessing Christians who have almost no prosperity. The things we are speaking of are some of the reasons why. Yes, go ahead and look at that new house or new car. Be believing for the things that you desire, but keep those things in their place.

When the house, car, etc. begins to take the place of God – taking up time and attention that belongs to Him – your prosperity will suffer.

Covetousness is a sneaky prosperity killer, often creeping into your life attached to the object of your faith. When you give too great a place to that car you're believing for, the thing that you thought *was* your prosperity begins to kill your prosperity. The things that you desire are likely not bad things in their place. The problem arises when they move beyond their place into God's place. We can ruin our own prosperity simply by turning our affections from God to the things that we desire. Don't let your prosperity kill your prosperity.

Do you remember the story of Abraham and Isaac? Abraham believed God for twenty-five years for a son. When he arrived, Isaac was the apple of Abraham's eye. It's quite possible that Isaac began to occupy a place in Abraham's life that used to be reserved for God. A major adjustment was needed to keep things in order. That adjustment came during the three-day hike up Mount Moriah, when Abraham offered his son to the Lord (Genesis 22). True, the physical sacrifice of Isaac didn't happen, but a heart-sacrifice did. Abraham reordered his priorities, keeping them in place from then on. He put God first.

IT'S NOT THE BOAT'S FAULT

I have often heard prosperity haters explain how luxury items are excessive and ungodly, and keep people from serving God. We can all agree that many have turned from God because of one hobby or another. Some moved from an apartment to a house and immediately began to spend Sunday mornings working on their lawn instead of worshipping God. Does that mean that apartments are better than houses, or that houses always keep people out of church? Obviously not. There are many homeowners who also manage to serve God. It's rarely the item itself that's the issue. The problem occurs when the person begins serving the thing instead of making sure the thing serves them.

> *No one can serve two masters, for either he will hate the one and love the other, or he will be devoted to the one and despise the other. You cannot serve God and money.*
>
> *Matthew 6:24*

When I pastored a church in New York State, we were blessed to own a lake home about an hour away. Along with the lake home, we owned the marina on the lake. Often we would spend weekends there, driving out on Friday afternoon, driving back in for church on Sunday, and then sometimes right back out to relax on Sunday afternoon. As we would leave to go to church, we would often pass a line of boaters launching their boats for the day. I would lament the fact that so many people were ignorant of the things of God, choosing to fish rather than worship.

One Sunday morning, as we were leaving and boaters were arriving, I heard the Lord speak this phrase in my spirit: *It's not the boat's fault.* I understood what He meant. Many would say that having a boat was the problem with these people, but really, failing to put God first (or simply not knowing Him) was the problem. At that time, I owned several boats, but was still able to make it to church every week. Physical items are neutral where God is concerned. Boats, motorcycles, sports cars, etc. neither hate God nor love Him.

Let's talk about a hypothetical family who is committed in church until they get a new boat. Now they can't make it to church because their friends want to go boating on Sunday mornings. The kids, who used to help serve in church, are now helping their dad carry cases of beer from the car out to the boat. Before long, marriage troubles surface, financial problems manifest (boats can be expensive to maintain), and the family falls apart. People in the church who know this family's plight may tell their friends, *Don't ever get a boat. That boat ruined their family.* No it didn't. Disobedience and stupidity ruined their family. Don't blame the boat. It's not the boat's fault.

Let's talk about another family. They are committed to the things of God and to the house of God. They are tithers and givers. As their kids are growing up, the parents have it in their heart to believe God for a boat. They sow some seed toward one, and eventually God leads them to a great deal on a barely used sport boat. They invite some friends from their neighborhood to go out on the lake with them the next Sunday, after church. On the boat, the conversation turns toward the things of God. Since there's no easy route of escape, the guests respectfully listen to the gospel and, right there in the middle of the lake, pray to receive Christ.

These brand new believers come to church the next Sunday,

meet many new brothers and sisters in the Lord, and watch as the things of God begin to transform their family. The same boat that ruined the first family blessed this family. The owners of the boat decide that this was too much fun not to repeat. They make a list of other friends and neighbors whom they can hold captive on the lake so they can fill the church up with new believers.

The boat, the house, the motorcycle, the car, the airplane, the horse – whatever it is that you enjoy – is not the issue. The issue is your heart. Some people are not able to handle these kinds of things; their walk with God would be compromised by having them. If that's the case with you, don't get these items. Stay away from that which would distract or pull you away from God. (I personally don't want anything that would pull me away from the Lord.) Possessions require maintenance. Maintenance means time and money. Things that you thought would enhance your life can end up controlling you.

It's important that we learn to think right about money and possessions. Things aren't the issue, the people who use them are the issue. It's not the boat's fault.

BE CAREFUL WHO YOU SHARE WITH

We must be careful how we talk about this subject, recognizing that people are at different levels of spirituality. While it's true that God wants us rich (and that Christ shed His blood to make it so), there are also other issues to consider. We must be sensitive to those whom we are with, looking to the Spirit for His leading. Understand that God intimately knows the condition of a person's heart. Although prosperity belongs to everyone, it's not always able to be received by everyone.

There have been several times during my ministry when I have begun to say something publicly about a possession that I had received, but sensed a check in my spirit not to proceed. Something on the inside of me told me not to talk about it at that time. As I thought about it later, I realized that one or more of the people gathered in the room may not have been able to understand, and a statement about a physical possession, especially an expensive one, could trip them up.

Some preachers might think, *Well I just believe in telling it like it is.* Go ahead, stupid. Cause your brother to stumble and see how long your ministry lasts. The Lord won't put up with that for long.

Others may think, *It sounds like you're being seeker sensitive.* I'm being Spirit-sensitive. We should all be sensitive to the Spirit's leadings as we minister, whether publicly, or one-on-one. We can lead people to a higher level, but we are not to force them there. When you force-feed someone, they end up choking and won't want to eat at your table anymore, spiritually speaking.

I don't share about all my blessings with everyone. There are times, as I mentioned, where I'm led to refrain from sharing about what God has done for me. At other times (while receiving an offering, for example) I have ended up spending the entire service sharing about how God brought certain things into my life. Because that was God's plan for the service, it helped everyone present and encouraged many to hold fast to their faith for God's best.

FIRST THINGS FIRST

We want to teach believers about prosperity, but claiming more possessions is usually not the first step the new believer needs to take. The first thing they need to learn is that, next to God, no person or possession comes close. They must learn to become dead to their fleshly desires and alive to God; to deny themselves, take up their cross, and follow Him.

A Christian who really wants to prosper must develop to the point where his or her possessions mean absolutely nothing. If a person knows the Lord, this shouldn't be an impossible task. What temporal possession or blessing is even close in value to Him? Not any. If you struggle with keeping your heart right in this area, believing God for a bigger house is not something that should even be on your radar. Spend time falling in love with Him until material possessions fade to the background.

A new believer can be more or less mature in these areas depending on what their life was like when they came to faith in Christ. Some people have been saturated with the vanities of this world and are self-absorbed and materialistic. It can take time for that person to believe that if God is all they have, they can make it (which is true). Because it takes time for that person to become free from their possessions, it will take time for them to move into the increase that God can bring. The Bible says much about these things.

Other people have little regard for possessions. When they

were in the world they didn't care about material things, and when they came to Christ, it was the same way. There is growth needed in different areas for this kind of individual. I was, in many ways, this type of person.

NO FURNITURE

As a young jazz musician, I needed my horns, my record albums, and a tuxedo to wear to work. That was pretty much it. Everything else was optional as far as I was concerned. When I got saved and got around certain Christians, they confirmed that my theology was indeed correct: if a person really loved God, there was no need for any of the things of this world. I spent my time learning that God was all I needed. I was young enough to have had few financial responsibilities, so lack was an adventure for me rather than a curse. I loved my quasi-bohemian lifestyle. I loved that everything I owned fit in my car. Then I met my wife. . . .

We had been dating for quite some time, and I was perfectly happy with that arrangement. The commitment level was in the low to medium range. I was on the road full time, didn't need an apartment or anything that would go in it, and was free to go as the Lord directed.

One day, my wife (then girlfriend) asked me where I thought our relationship was headed. I didn't think it was headed anywhere. I was enjoying living for the *now*. Then she asked if I ever thought we would marry. No, I had never thought about that. I wasn't sure I wanted to think about that.

She put me on the spot with that question and, although I usually enjoyed being around her, I was uncomfortable with where this conversation was going. My response to her went something like this: *You don't want to marry me. If you marry me, you'll want a nice place to live. I'll never have a nice place to live because I'm called to serve God. If, somehow, we did get a nice place to live, you'd want furniture to go in it. Furniture is expensive. I'll never be able to buy you nice furniture because I'm serving God. So, you don't want to marry me.* That was my take on our future. At least I was honest.

I can't explain why she didn't leave me that day. (Or any of the other times over the next several months until we married.) We have been married now for many years and have nice houses. And some furniture.

The point I'm illustrating is this: my big issue was not that I needed deliverance from my possessions. I needed deliverance from wrong thinking and small believing. I needed to learn what God had provided for me, that serving God was not akin to a vow of poverty, and that I should consider my wife's desires, not just my own. That was me. Another person may come to Christ consumed with material possessions, an issue quite opposite of mine.

Can you see why the scriptures address both the *blessing* side of prosperity and the *leave all and follow Him* side? We need it all. The Christian who only views one side of the mountain will never enjoy God's full prosperity.

Chapter 6
GOD'S OPERATING SYSTEM

Sell your possessions, and give to the needy. Provide your-selves with moneybags that do not grow old, with a treasure in the heavens that does not fail, where no thief approaches and no moth destroys. For where your treasure is, there will your heart be also.

Luke 12:33-34

There is more than one side to this subject of prosperity. This has been stated repeatedly, however, not understanding this one fact causes many lives to be troubled and, in some cases, destroyed. Because many have only been exposed to one side of this truth, some believe that the Bible teaches prosperity, while others believe that the Bible is against prosperity. Let me set the record straight: the Bible teaches prosperity, period. In doing so, the Bible also brings stern warnings about how to handle money and possessions. We must heed those warnings if we are to prosper.

Jesus said some things about money and finances that could cause prosperity believers to scratch their heads in wonderment. The passage above is one such instance. We'll discuss this passage in a moment, but first let's agree on something: the Bible – all of the Bible – is true and right. We need not fear any portion of Scripture, for the Word of God is perfect (Psalms 19:7). Even though some passages may, on the surface, appear to be speaking against prosperity, I have found this to be true: *every* passage is a prosperity passage.

In my book, *The Coming of the Lord*, I go into some detail about the importance of properly interpreting Scripture. When reading a passage, one of the questions that we must always ask is, *Who is speaking, and to whom are they speaking?* We ask that question because these things matter. We, believers in Christ, are the Church, and must give the greatest weight to those things which are spoken to the Church. Things that are spoken to other people groups can still bring us valuable instruction, but we must weigh those things against what has been spoken directly to us.

In this passage in Luke 12, Jesus was speaking. But to whom was He speaking? He was speaking to two types of people: His followers, and many potential followers (today we would call them new believers and seekers). None of these people, however, were born again; they lived primarily in the natural realm, functioning in this world's system. These people needed to turn their hearts away from the natural – away from possessions – and onto the things of God. Look again at the last phrase in this passage:

For where your treasure is, there will your heart be also.

Luke 12:34

Jesus was preparing their hearts for a major adjustment: a new way of living. He wasn't teaching them that they were destined for a life of poverty. Rather, He was helping them receive a proper perspective where temporal blessings are concerned. He was helping them see that, although prosperity includes things, things are not prosperity. None of these people were mature enough in Christ to learn the deeper principles of abundance because none of them were yet in Christ. They needed truth at the most elementary level.

Many of those who oppose prosperity use passages like this to support their views that money is evil, and that prosperity is a curse rather than a blessing. They miss it, however, by not discerning whom Jesus was speaking to (not the Church), and by not reading the rest of the passage. Let's take a moment to look at several of the preceding verses that are part of this same passage:

And he said to his disciples, "Therefore I tell you, do not be anxious about your life, what you will eat, nor about your body, what you will put on. For life is more than food, and the body more than clothing. Consider the ravens: they neither sow nor reap, they have neither storehouse nor barn, and yet God feeds them. Of how much more value are you than the birds! And which of you by being anxious can add a single hour to his span of life? If then you are not able to do as small a thing as that, why are you anxious about the rest? Consider the lilies, how they grow: they neither toil nor spin, yet I tell you, even Solomon in all his glory was not arrayed like one of these. But if God so clothes the grass, which is alive in the field today, and tomorrow is thrown into the oven, how much more will he clothe you, O you of little faith! And do not seek

what you are to eat and what you are to drink, nor be wor-
ried. For all the nations of the world seek after these things,
and your Father knows that you need them. Instead, seek his
kingdom, and these things will be added to you. ***Fear not, lit-***
tle flock, for it is your Father's good pleasure to give you the
kingdom. *Sell your possessions, and give to the needy. Pro-*
vide yourselves with moneybags that do not grow old, with
a treasure in the heavens that does not fail, where no thief
approaches and no moth destroys. For where your treasure is,
there will your heart be also.

Luke 12:22-34

This passage isn't teaching against prosperity at all (although people with a glass-half-empty mentality will still manage to see it that way). Rather, Jesus is showing us how much God desires to take care of us, and how easily it can happen.

THE KINGDOM OF GOD

The key to understanding this passage is found in the phrase *the Kingdom of God*, a subject with which the Body of Christ needs to become better acquainted. Most believe that the King-dom of God is a reference to our eternal destination in Heaven. Not at all. The Kingdom of God is our way of life here on Earth. Here's an illustration to help us understand God's kingdom:

I usually write my books on my laptop computer, but I am writing this book on a new tablet-style computer that I pur-chased. With a keyboard attached, it's similar to my laptop, yet it runs on a different operating system. I can't do everything on the tablet exactly like I would do it on the laptop because it's just not designed to work that way. Because the operating systems are different, I must learn the similarities and differences between the two machines. In the same way, God's way of doing things is different than ours, even though similarities exist.

The Kingdom of God is God's operating system – the way He works – His way of doing things. By contrast, there is also *the kingdom of this world* (Revelation 11:15). That's the world's operating system.

Jesus said, *Fear not, little flock, for it is your Father's good pleasure to give you the kingdom* (Luke 12:32). He's saying, in essence, *Don't be concerned about where things are going to come from. God's going to show you how to get what you need so you'll always have plenty.* Jesus was helping us move away from the kingdom of this world and into God's kingdom where we do things the way He does them.

When speaking of provision being added to us, Jesus said the Father would give us *the kingdom*. Notice that He didn't say the Father would give us food and clothing. Those things come as we seek the kingdom, learning to function in God's operating system. God doesn't rain down food and clothes from Heaven for us, He shows us how to operate the laws of His kingdom to receive what we need.

Some of the laws of God's kingdom are similar to the laws of this world's kingdom. Others are completely different. For example, in God's kingdom we love our enemies instead of hating them. We pray for those who curse us instead of cursing them back. Choosing to operate in God's kingdom instead of the world's system will always bring a desired result.

Where prosperity and provision are concerned, the world's system teaches us to store up and hold tight to our possessions in order to increase. God's kingdom, on the other hand, teaches us to release our money and goods. His kingdom is a different way of doing things that yields greater results.

With this in mind, the last two verses in this passage make a bit more sense.

> *Sell your possessions, and give to the needy. Provide yourselves with moneybags that do not grow old, with a treasure in the heavens that does not fail, where no thief approaches and no moth destroys. For where your treasure is, there will your heart be also.*
>
> *Luke 12:33-34*

When Jesus told His crowd that day to sell what they had and give to the poor, it wasn't a recipe for long-term poverty. Rather, He was jump-starting them in the laws of the Kingdom by encouraging them to get some good seed in the ground. He was positioning them for increase.

I'll say it again: *Every* scripture is a prosperity scripture. All of the Word brings increase. In every case, the passages that people use to preach against prosperity are actually teaching prosperity. Let's look at another passage in this same chapter.

> *And he said to them, "Take care, and be on your guard against all covetousness, for one's life does not consist in the abundance of his possessions." And he told them a parable,*

saying, "*The land of a rich man produced plentifully, and he thought to himself, What shall I do, for I have nowhere to store my crops?' And he said, 'I will do this: I will tear down my barns and build larger ones, and there I will store all my grain and my goods. And I will say to my soul, "Soul, you have ample goods laid up for many years; relax, eat, drink, be merry."' But God said to him, Fool! This night your soul is required of you, and the things you have prepared, whose will they be?' So is the one who lays up treasure for himself and is not rich toward God."*

Luke 12:15-21

Prosperity is more than just the accumulation of possessions. (I'm sorry if you believed otherwise.) Possessions are simply the byproduct of prosperity.

Jesus told us in this passage, *Be on your guard against all covetousness.* Are we practicing this verse, or does it just apply to the anti-prosperity crowd? If we desire prosperity, we had better pay attention to verses like these. Covetousness – putting people and things before God – is prevalent in the Body of Christ. We cannot afford to disqualify ourselves from the prosperity that God has for us. We need it, because He needs it. He needs the world's resources in the hands of His Body where He can direct them.

Let's talk for a moment about this man who made the dubious decision to tear down his barns and build new ones. This man had a bumper crop. What's so bad about a good crop? Absolutely nothing. The issue wasn't that he had a good crop, it's that he had a wrong heart. He let his material prosperity determine His life's direction instead of letting God lead Him through life. We are never to allow circumstances, good or bad, to move us off the principles of the Word and the leading of the Spirit.

There's two phrases in this passage that give us a clear picture of what was going on. Notice the phrase, *He thought to himself*. If people would only think less and believe more, they wouldn't get in so much trouble. A person's unrenewed mind will lead them astray every single time. We must take time daily to feed on God's thoughts (God's Word contains God's thoughts), making His thoughts our own. Right thinking would have helped this man seek God for His plan instead of just operating according to the world's system.

The second key to this passage is found in the word *relax*. This man's relaxing was his undoing. Is God opposed to relaxation? Of course not. We all need down time where we enjoy ourselves and take it easy. The relaxing that this man was doing, however, was different. He was spiritually relaxed – lax, we might say – toward the things of God, turning from the God-realm, and gravitating toward the earthly-realm. His relaxed attitude toward the things of God caused him to default to the lower kingdom of this world instead of seeking the Kingdom of God.

Remember, in the Kingdom of God, one of the main ways we increase is by sowing. This man wasn't interested in sowing; he was just interested in storing and saving. One good crop, and he was ready to retire, buy an RV, and see the sights. That kind of life is not prosperity if God's not in it. Sure, there may be a time when it's right to build a bigger barn, but we must realize that the Kingdom of God works the most when things are in motion, not when they're still (read James 5:3). As we read earlier, we are not to let our moneybags grow old (Luke 12:33).

There's another important issue that should be discussed here. We are not to act as though our money is our own. It's really not. A believer may have great possessions, own businesses, and have a lot of money in the bank, but who owns the believer? Last I checked, I was not my own, but rather belonged to the Lord (1 Corinthians 6:20). If He's my Lord – my Master – than all of my money is really His. I don't just make my own financial decisions, rather, I seek the Lord for His plan. The man in this passage kept the Lord out of his plans: a very unwise decision. The only reason we have what we have is because of the Lord.

Notice that this man's problems had nothing to do with farming skills, or business skills. His lack of spiritual skill was the issue. Wrong thinking killed his prosperity, causing him to set his affection on things on the earth rather than on things above (Colossians 3:2). If we want to prosper, we must think right about money and possessions, keeping them in their proper place.

Notice again the last phrase in this passage:

So is the one who lays up treasure for himself and is not rich toward God.

Luke 12:21

Saving, or laying up treasure for ourselves, is not a bad thing (most of us need to save more). Laying up treasure for ourselves while not being rich toward God is the issue. Are you rich in your fellowship with Him, or do you and He barely speak? Are you passionate in your relationship, or could you honestly care less? Are you free with your giving, putting His works first, or do you just drop an empty envelope in the plate while thinking, *I got away with keeping it again?* People disqualify for prosperity in these very simple areas.

We're still talking about the prosperity killer called covetousness. When people lay up treasure for themselves and are not rich toward God, they are practicing idolatry. Such people don't need to claim a new wardrobe, or add to their classic car collection. They need to sell some of what they have and give some things away. Less distractions and fewer obligations are needed. They need to learn to function in God's Kingdom where He is everything, and everything else is secondary.

Chapter 7

THE LOVE OF MONEY

Teach these things, Timothy, and encourage everyone to obey them. Some people may contradict our teaching, but these are the wholesome teachings of the Lord Jesus Christ. These teachings promote a godly life. Anyone who teaches something different is arrogant and lacks understanding. Such a person has an unhealthy desire to quibble over the meaning of words. This stirs up arguments ending in jealousy, division, slander, and evil suspicions. These people always cause trouble. Their minds are corrupt, and they have turned their backs on the truth. To them, a show of godliness is just a way to become wealthy. Yet true godliness with contentment is itself great wealth. After all, we brought nothing with us when we came into the world, and we can't take anything with us when we leave it. So if we have enough food and clothing, let us be content. But people who long to be rich fall into temptation and are trapped by many foolish and harmful desires that plunge them into ruin and destruction. For the love of money is the root of all kinds of evil. And some people, craving money, have wandered from the true faith and pierced themselves with many sorrows.

1 Timothy 6:2-10 (NLT)

This passage – a favorite of prosperity opponents – causes many believers to question whether prosperity is right. We know the answer to that question: every passage is a prosperity passage. Prosperity is indeed right.

Paul was writing to Timothy, the young pastor of the church at Ephesus. He was instructing him to stay with what he had been taught, and was helping him identify the kind of people who would be problem-causers in the church. The people that Paul was talking about here are not your normal church members, but the kind who come into a church for the purpose of taking advantage of people. They are ungodly and depraved: not the kind of people who qualify for prosperity. If you happen to see yourself in the passage above or the verse below, repent at once and turn to God.

> *and constant friction among people who are depraved in mind and deprived of the truth, imagining that godliness is a means of gain.*
>
> 1 Timothy 6:5

Opponents of prosperity use this verse to try and discredit all prosperity teaching. They say, *Prosperity preachers want you to believe that if you'll just do certain things, you'll prosper, but this verse shows us that's not true.* No it doesn't. People who say such things are taking this verse out of its setting, assigning a different meaning than God intended. They vilify prosperity preachers (people who preach the Word of God), accusing them of manipulating the scriptures to connect godliness with material wealth. We don't need to manipulate anything to equate serving God with wealth, we just need to read the next verse:

> *But godliness with contentment is **great gain**.*
>
> 1 Timothy 6:6

Godliness – living according to the laws of the Kingdom of God – is indeed a recipe for increase. This verse is not saying that every Christian who lives for God will automatically become wealthy, nor is it implying that every wealthy person is godly. It is saying something tremendous, however: the result of godliness is increase. Great gain. That phrase thrills me. Look at this verse in *The Amplified Bible*:

> *[And it is, indeed, a source of **immense profit**, for] godliness accompanied with contentment (that contentment which is a sense of inward sufficiency) is **great and abundant gain**.*

Immense profit. Great and abundant gain. What precious promises! Is the profit and gain spoken of here only financial? That's doubtful, but any increase from God is a welcome addition to my life. We again find that the verses that many use to try and disprove prosperity are actually proclaiming prosperity.

FLEECING THE FLOCK

1 Timothy 6:5 was never meant to be an indictment against prosperity preachers, unless those preachers are like the people described in the first part of the verse: *depraved in mind and deprived of the truth*. This verse (and the surrounding passage) should never describe any preacher (or any Christian, for that matter). Yes, there have been a handful of charlatans who have violated God's flock for their own gain, but we are not to discount the faithfulness of the many because of the unfaithfulness of a few. There have also been investment bankers who stole

from their investors. Do we stop investing because of the indiscretions of a few? No. Nor do we cease preaching God's Word on prosperity because of the missteps of a few. The behavior of a minister, unfortunate as it may be, has absolutely no bearing upon the written Word of God. We don't change our beliefs because somebody was unfaithful with money.

Look at *The Message* translation of verse five:

They think religion is a way to make a fast buck.

If any preacher tells you that sowing a special seed into his ministry will cause something miraculous to happen for you in the next few days or weeks, run the other way. That preacher wants something to happen fast for him, not for you. The only thing that will happen fast for you is falling behind financially. There's nothing fast about true prosperity. The prosperity of God manifests over the long-term in the lives of those who faithfully serve Him and practice His principles.

Don't misunderstand me. There have been many times when God has dealt with me to sow a substantial seed into a person or ministry, and to sow it quickly. In many of those cases, I received a quick harvest of blessing in return. It makes all the difference when God is in it.

THE LOVE OF MONEY

But those who desire to be rich fall into temptation, into a snare, into many senseless and harmful desires that plunge people into ruin and destruction. For the love of money is a root of all kinds of evils. It is through this craving that some have wandered away from the faith and pierced themselves with many pangs.

1 Timothy 6:9-10

There is nothing – absolutely nothing – in this passage that teaches that money is evil, or that being rich will ruin your life. You must choose to leave out certain key words in this passage and ignore many others to conclude such things. Prosperity haters do just that. Prominent leaders in the Body of Christ use this passage to teach that riches will cause the believer to become suicidal (I'm not exaggerating), and that money will cause people to leave the faith. Rubbish. That kind of teaching is pure garbage. I don't normally make such harsh statements, but this kind of religious teaching tripped me up for many years.

I came into Christianity from a Jewish background, where our heritage and identity taught us to expect to do well in life. Not until I came among Christians did I learn to think small and have nothing (remember the furniture story?). I had for so long embraced the lie that it was wrong to have anything, that I was indeed afraid to have anything. That fear kept me from ever reaching for more. I would give freely and sow faithfully, but was afraid that a great harvest would keep me from serving God.

I had been hearing messages and studying about prosperity for a number of years, yet the foundation of small thinking that I had received in my first church was still in place. It took years to dig up that false foundation and replace it with the truth.

I'll never forget the day my deliverance came. I had been working as a staff member for a large ministry. One day, while driving home for lunch, I noticed a change in my spirit. That fear of prospering that I had carried around for years was gone: kicked out by the Word of God. At that moment, I knew that I could be extremely blessed and still serve God all the way. Tears streamed down my face as I rejoiced in the change that God had worked in me. From that day to this, although I stay on guard against covetousness, I haven't been afraid to be as blessed as I can be.

If, as the verse says, people are *plunged into ruin and destruction* and *wander from the faith*, it's not because of money, it's because those people chose to serve money instead of God. Money itself is neutral. It's a magnifier. It can make a wicked man more wicked and it can make a godly man more of a blessing. If riches ruin someone, it's not the fault of the money. (It's not the boat's fault, remember?) When the verse speaks of those who desire to be rich, it's talking about a person who craves money, making riches their pursuit. I don't pursue money, I pursue God. I am rich, not because I lust after riches, but because God, through Christ's poverty, has made me rich.

Money is not the root of all evil, the *love* of money is. *The love of money* refers to greed and unwholesome desires, not a Christian who is standing in faith, believing God for provision. Are some Christians motivated by greed? I imagine so. Such people need to forget about possessions and just draw close to God. As for me, I refuse to love money. I do require a lot of it to do what

I'm called to do, therefore I believe God for plenty of money to come in. I've passed up many opportunities to follow after money, and will likely have to pass up many more. So will you.

CONTENTMENT

One verse in particular in our passage in 1 Timothy seems, at first glance, to teach that the believer should turn from prosperity, seeking instead to live a more base existence. We must be willing to take an honest look at this verse to discover God's intended meaning.

> *But if we have food and clothing, with these we will be content.*
>
> *1 Timothy 6:8*

Certain words in Scripture have one meaning in our English vernacular, but another meaning altogether when used in the Bible. The word *love*, for example, can have a very different meaning in our language than we see in Scripture. The phrase, *I just love your outfit*, does not convey the same depth of meaning as the phrase, *for God so loved the world*. Another example: the word *peace* in our society means an absence of conflict, but the peace of God is a settledness that exists regardless of conflict. These words share the same basic meanings, yet a closer look reveals important differences. The same is true for the word *content*.

When we use the word *contentment* in our language, we often use it interchangeably with the word *satisfaction*. A person who is satisfied has no desire for anything more or greater. They're happy to stay right where they are.

If contentment means that I'm not supposed to desire anything greater than my present circumstances, we have a big problem. Too many other scriptures teach us to reach out, press in, move forward, and dream big. Although I'm thankful for basic provision, I know too much about God to just be satisfied with a plate of food and a shirt on my back. I have a family to take care of and ministries to support. I need to go places and do things as He directs. Walking everywhere won't cut it for me.

Fortunately, in the scriptures, the word *content* has a deeper meaning.

The Bible definition of *content* means that my heart is undisturbed by the circumstances around me. If I have nothing but food and clothes, I may not be satisfied, but nor am I disturbed. When you read *content* in the Bible, think *undisturbed*. Notice how Paul, who wrote this passage in 1 Timothy, used this same word elsewhere:

> *I rejoiced in the Lord greatly that now at length you have revived your concern for me. You were indeed concerned for me, but you had no opportunity. Not that I am speaking of being in need, for **I have learned in whatever situation I am to be content**. I know how to be brought low, and I know how to abound. In any and every circumstance, I have learned the secret of facing plenty and hunger, abundance and need. I can do all things through him who strengthens me. Yet it was kind of you to share my trouble. Philippians 4:10-14*

If the word *content* meant the same thing as *satisfied*, Paul should have gotten upset when the Philippian's offering showed up to change his circumstances. Instead, he rejoiced. He wasn't satisfied with his situation, in fact, he called the lack that he was experiencing *trouble*. Paul was content – undisturbed and unmoved – in the midst of lack and financial trouble. Although not satisfied with his present circumstances, he was able to remain stable and in peace. If that's what contentment means, I'll take it.

We are to be content – undisturbed – in our present circumstances, even if our present circumstances are not our desired circumstances. Many fall short in this regard. Too many believers think that they are not prosperous until they arrive at a certain level of income or live in a certain type of home. They are unhappy with their circumstances and live in frustration. They don't realize that prosperity is only an attitude adjustment away. If a person will learn to be content, he or she can prosper right where they are, at every level.

Many say they are believing God, when they are really agitated and discontent. That's not prosperity and it's not faith. If a person is not content, they're not in faith, and if they're not in faith, their circumstances will not change. It can be frustrating when negative circumstances arise, but we must not allow frustration to move us. Frustration is not faith.

Faith maintains peace even in the most difficult times. Do you remember the Shunnamite woman who ministered to Elisha? When her child suddenly died, she ran to Elisha for help. When he asked her what was wrong, she replied, *All is well* (2

Kings 4:23). She wasn't denying the existence of troubling circumstances, but was, rather, denying those circumstances the right to trouble her heart. Learn to be okay on the inside, no matter where you are, regardless of circumstance. Enjoy the ride through every stage and phase of life, and God will always see you through to victory, as He did the Shunnamite woman. Her child was raised back to life.

To be content does not mean you are satisfied *ultimately*, it means you are functioning well in an uncomfortable place *temporarily*. Why would anyone go through lack with a smile on their face? Because their faith has already laid hold of their provision. Paul, in verse 12, said he had *learned the secret of facing plenty and hunger, abundance and need*. What is this secret that he had learned? When circumstances change, you don't. If you won't change, the circumstances will. Learn to be happy and undisturbed where you are, while reaching for more. That's contentment.

> *Keep your life free from love of money, and* **be content** *with what you have, for he has said, "I will never leave you nor forsake you."*
>
> *Hebrews 13:5*

Again, at first glance, it would seem as though this verse is saying, *Don't reach for more, don't desire better.* That's what it does say to the person who only reads the first half of the verse. Read the rest of it. We are able to be content with what we have, because our Provider is ever with us and won't forsake us. To *forsake* means *to give up on something or someone.* God, our Provider, will never do that. He doesn't just say, *I'm with you,* while watching you spiral down the drain. He's with us, bless God, to provide for us! He wants to be all that He is, all the time, to us.

Looking at the next verse in this passage brings even more clarity:

So we can confidently say, "The Lord is my helper; I will not fear; what can man do to me?"

Hebrews 13:6

If being content means (as many believe) that we just back down, back off, and *settle for our lot in life,* then verse 6 is really out of place. This passage shows the opposite of someone who is backing down. When the All-sufficient One – the Provider who sees ahead – is with us, we are able to look contradicting circumstances in the face and boldly declare, *I'll not fear lack and I'll not fear man. The Lord is with me to help me!* As long as I have Him, I'm content: undisturbed and unmoved.

We have seen three passages that teach us to be content (not satisfied) in our present circumstances. If those circumstances are unfavorable, they will change as we remain in a place of contentment and faith. While wisely warning against the perils of covetousness, none of these passages teach what many suggest: that we are to simply accept life's circumstances, withdrawing from the desires that God has birthed within us.

If indeed Paul, in 1 Timothy 6, was teaching that we should shun material prosperity, he ruined his point by something he said just a few verses later:

As for the rich in this present age, charge them not to be haughty, nor to set their hopes on the uncertainty of riches, but on God, **who richly provides us with everything to enjoy.**

1 Timothy 6:17

This verse shows the balance of the different sides of prosperity. On one side, we are cautioned against allowing our possessions to influence us, pulling us away from God into a place of deception. On the other side, we see God's abundant provision, His unchanging desire for our enjoyment. Let's embrace both sides of prosperity, avoiding covetousness, the great prosperity killer.

Chapter 8

STINGINESS

PROSPERITY KILLER #2: STINGINESS

The point is this: whoever sows sparingly will also reap sparingly, and whoever sows bountifully will also reap bountifully. Each one must give as he has decided in his heart, not reluctantly or under compulsion, for God loves a cheerful giver.

2 Corinthians 9:6-7

This passage is of great importance to the believer who desires prosperity, for it illustrates the truth that, with God, it's not just *what* we do that matters but *how* we do it. Although the Bible emphasizes giving, it also draws a distinction between the gift and the heart of the giver. Giving is much more than a financial transaction. It's also a spiritual act – part of our worship – the amount of the gift being secondary to the spiritual attributes. Two people could bring gifts of an identical amount, yet God would see them very differently because of how they gave it.

Some would argue, *Why confuse things or make it harder for people? Isn't it enough that they gave?* If a person's heart isn't right they really didn't give, even though money may have changed hands. God deems giving to have occurred when the gift comes from a right heart; He pays more attention to the heart than the amount. We see this illustrated in this passage from the ministry of Jesus:

*And he sat down opposite the treasury and watched the people putting money into the offering box. Many rich people put in large sums. And a poor widow came and put in two small copper coins, which make a penny. And he called his disciples to him and said to them, "Truly, I say to you, **this poor widow has put in more than all** those who are contributing to the offering box. For they all contributed out of their abundance, but she out of her poverty has put in everything she had, all she had to live on."*

Mark 12:41-44

There are many things to observe here. First, notice that Jesus sat there watching the offering. It would be safe to conclude that He still watches offerings today. Offerings are more than just a necessary item of business, they are a spiritual act of worship as we gather together. God is in the midst of the offering, just as Jesus was on this day. We need a greater revelation of the offerings of the Lord.

On this day, we see rich people giving large offerings, and this lady, who gave what most would consider an insignificant offering. Far from being insignificant, however, Jesus identified her's as the biggest of the day. People didn't have checkbooks or debit cards back then, so you could tell roughly what a person was giving by how many coins they brought. Some might require a bag for their offering. This woman's gift was minuscule: no bag required.

Jesus was looking at more than just bags of money. (The verse said He was watching the people, it didn't say He was watching the money.) He wasn't just looking at what they brought, He was looking at how they brought it. It wasn't just that the widow's gift stood out to Him, the widow's *giving* was also impressive.

We see an important lesson here. A large sum doesn't make an offering big, and a small sum doesn't make an offering small. It's the heart behind the offering that determines what kind of seed was sown. I imagine that some of the rich folks just tossed their tithe-bags in the box rather nonchalantly, like they would pay a bill (that's how many give today). This woman, on the other hand, gave with faith and purpose. How do we know? You don't give your last cent unless you really mean it.

Although the rich gave large amounts, it's possible that they gave *sparingly*, with a small heart and tight fist. This poor woman, on the other hand, although she only had the smallest amount, gave *bountifully*, or freely. *Sparingly* and *bountifully*. These words mean much where prosperity is concerned. They are not just indicators of dollar amounts, but rather of conditions of the heart.

Let's go back to 2 Corinthians 9:6, looking at it in a few other translations:

Remember: A stingy planter gets a stingy crop; a lavish planter gets a lavish crop. (Message)

All I will say is that poor sowing means a poor harvest, and generous sowing means a generous harvest. (Phillips)

POOR SOWING

Sparingly, stingy, poor. These are heavy words indeed when describing a person's heart. The word translated as *sparingly,* found only in this verse, means to *forgo*. To forgo means *to skip* or *go without*. Someone might say, *I'm going to forgo dessert tonight*. That's another way of saying, *I'm going to sit this one out*. If someone gives sparingly, they obviously gave. However, there's a sense in which they chose to *sit this one out*. They may have put their money in, but they kept their heart out of the transaction. Here's the problem with that: if you *sit this one out* when it's time to sow, you will *sit this one out* when it's time to reap.

If the heart is not engaged, the offering, whatever the amount, is one that is given *poorly* (as the *Phillips* translation says). Poor sowing makes for poor reaping, and is a big reason why there are so many poor Christians. One simply cannot sow sparingly and reap bountifully. There's no such thing as poor sowing and a rich harvest.

Another good definition for *sparingly* is *to hold back*. A person can hold back what they should give. And, as we have said, they can give, but hold back their heart. We want to be bountiful, generous givers rather than being narrow, stingy givers. Stinginess is a prosperity killer.

Stinginess is a smallness of heart: a narrow, constricted opening on the inside of a person through which they release as little as possible. It's the spiritual version of blocked arteries. Blocked arteries are a serious condition in one's physical heart, and stinginess is just as serious when found in man's spirit. Why is stinginess such a big deal? Because the small, pin-sized opening of heart through which the stingy person gives is the same opening through which they receive. Sow sparingly, reap sparingly.

The stingy person reaps sparingly, forgoing the blessing of God. This is not because God is mad at the person and wants to punish them for their Scrooge-like attitude. Rather, they simply don't have the capacity of heart to receive what God has given. The blessings of God are too grand to fit through openings as small as the one in the stingy person's heart.

I know person after person who has lived their whole life with little. They might attribute their poverty to the economy, lack of education, or a failure of the government to take care of them. However, the real reason they always had little is because they were little. They were narrow, constricted, penny-pinching, stingy souls who held back all they could, skipped every opportunity they had to be generous, and chose to sit out the many harvests that could have been theirs. No, they weren't bad people, or even mean people. They were just narrow in their thinking, and small in their believing. They refused to change any of it, even after hearing the truth that would enlarge and set them free.

Some of these same people would get mad if they saw someone else receiving financial or material blessings. They would choke over the blessings in other people's lives because the opening in their heart wasn't big enough to take it in. I experienced some of these things while pastoring a church in one of the poorest regions in the nation. The poverty of our region was firmly fixed in the hearts of many of our people.

Don't misunderstand me. You can hear the Word of God just one time and it can rearrange your entire life, setting things in order. Most people, however, don't have what Jesus called *ears to hear.* The smallness of heart that keeps them living with little also keeps them from receiving the revelation from the Word that would enlarge them.

THE PREACHER'S HOUSE

While I was pastoring, God blessed us with a lovely home. Some of our people were offended by it, leaving the church before we could even move in. There was nothing ultra extravagant about our home. It was a moderately sized, older home that actually needed a lot of work (I woke up early one morning to the sound of our ceiling falling down due to a leaky roof). People who are used to taking care of a pastor would think absolutely nothing of a house like ours. People who are stingy, however, choke on almost anything.

We lived in that home for a few years, and took great care of it. One day, as we were completing one of the final rehab projects, the Lord spoke to my spirit and said, *Get this house ready to sell.* What? We really enjoyed this house, having just remodeled it from top to bottom. Plus, it was paid for. We were open to being stretched, however, if that's what the Lord wanted. The Lord showed us what He had in mind for us and, by His grace, got us into it when everything around us said we couldn't.

Our church wasn't very large, and we knew that people would eventually find out about our new home, so I went ahead and shared with them how God had led us. Many were excited but, as expected, the small thinkers choked and left. They got mad. They said they were mad at my house, but they were really mad at *their* house. They were upset that things had changed for us, while nothing was changing for them. We can readily see why things weren't changing for them: they were stingy. I was walking in prosperity while they were killing theirs.

Someone may think, *I thought you said that we must not choke people; that we should be sensitive, being careful what we share.* Yes, that's true, but these people – every one of them – had sat under our teaching for years. None of these who got mad were seekers or new believers. All were people who had been saved a long time but had refused to grow up. We are indeed to be led with what we share, but there are times when God will lead you to tell it even if it causes someone to leave.

Most of our people rejoiced when the Lord brought us into larger places. They knew that if they kept following the Word we were following, the same things could happen for them, and for many, it did. If it had meant the salvation or growth of just one person, I would have been willing not to move to a bigger home. God led me to it, however, so I obeyed. We want to help everyone we can, but some people are going to resist change, choosing to remain stingy.

RELUCTANT GIVERS

Each one must give as he has decided in his heart, not reluctantly or under compulsion, for God loves a cheerful giver.
2 Corinthians 9:7

A person cannot sow sparingly and reap bountifully. In the same way, one cannot sow reluctantly and reap bountifully. This verse tells us that we are not to give *reluctantly or under compulsion.*

To give reluctantly means a person is giving when they really don't want to. This verse tells us not to do that. Either make the heart adjustment to become willing, or don't give. God does not accept the unwilling gift. As ministers, we should not try to force people to do what they don't want to do. We can, however, teach people how to give with a right heart.

I've had people help me with different projects before. Some of them had told me, *If you ever need help, please let me know.* When I needed help I let them know. Sometimes they would show up, but it was obvious that they didn't really want to be there. I purposed not to call those people again, because I don't want help from people who don't want to be there. I also don't want gifts from people who don't want to give them.

GRUDGE MONEY

*Don't eat with people who are stingy; don't desire their delicacies. **They are always thinking about how much it costs.** "Eat and drink," they say, but they don't mean it.*

Proverbs 23:6-7 (NLT)

I don't want someone taking me out to dinner who sits there complaining about the prices the whole time. I've had such experiences. I purposely left an item in the booth after the meal so I had an excuse to run back to the table. I did that so I could leave more tip money. The person I was with was so cheap that I knew they would short-change the server.

I don't want grudge gifts or grudge money. I don't want an offering that has to be pried out of the people's hands. God is no different. He doesn't want the unwilling gift. He wants you to *want to*.

COMPULSION

*Each one must give as he has decided in his heart, not reluctantly **or under compulsion**, for God loves a cheerful giver.*
2 Corinthians 9:7

Reluctance speaks of giving when you don't want to. *Compulsion* is when someone is twisting your arm, making you feel like you have to.

I've said it already, but I'll say it again: you don't have to give. If you have to, it's not giving, it's paying. I pay taxes under compulsion. I pay my bills under compulsion. I do not give under compulsion.

As ministers, we must exercise caution in this area. It's easy to feel the pressure of the needs of the ministry and pass that pressure on to the people, making them feel as though they must give. That's compulsion. The quickest way to get someone to not want to do something is to make them feel as though they must do it. When I have to do it, it can no longer come from the heart. I don't know about you, but I give the most when I *want* to give. I don't respond well to pressure.

There is another side to this truth. As a believer, I do have financial responsibilities toward my church. From *my* perspective as a believer, I have to give, but it's not because someone is forcing me. I have to give in the same way that I have to eat. I eat because I'm hungry and want to eat. I give because I'm hungry to see the plan of God advance and want to give. If ministers will teach the Word in this area instead of applying pressure to their congregation, the people will want to give. Any person that receives a full revelation of this truth will practically beg to give. They will pray for the preacher to stop talking and pass the plate. They would rush the platform with their gifts. Notice how this very thing happened in the Early Church:

> For they gave according to their means, as I can testify, and beyond their means, of their own accord, **begging us earnestly** for the favor of taking part in the relief of the saints.
>
> *2 Corinthians 8:3-4*

One time, I attended a service featuring a guest minister. I had an idea ahead of time what I would likely give in the offering: a respectable, generous amount. This minister received his own offering, taking some time to look in the Word. As he preached, he brought forth the Word with such skill that it came up in my heart to quadruple my offering; I was getting so thrilled with the Word that he was preaching. However, before collecting the offering, that preacher paused to show a video about his ministry. Something about that video seemed like it was produced for the purpose of raising funds. As the video progressed, the Spirit stirred my heart again, saying, *Just give the original amount you had planned to give.*

On one hand, I was shocked to have heard that, yet, at the

same time, I wasn't. Giving in response to the Word is scriptural. Giving in response to an emotional presentation is not. Whether intentioned or not, the pressure to do something in response to the video was there. That video would have been fine to show during another part of the service, but not right before the offering. We must remember what Jesus told Brother Hagin: *Be very careful about money.* That's not just speaking about being careful how you spend it. We must be careful to accurately represent the Lord when representing Him to others.

STINGY MARRIAGES

Stinginess is not just something that manifests during the offering in church services. Stingy people are selfish all the time. Married couples can sometimes be stingy toward each other, always keeping track and keeping tabs. They always know who did what when, and for whom. *Well, you just got this, so I should be able to get this. Well, three years ago you got this.* I absolutely despise that kind of talk. I hate hearing married couples talk about marriage being a fifty-fifty proposition. Baloney. That's ungodly. Husbands are told to give their whole life for their wives (Ephesians 5:25). That sounds like giving one hundred percent, not fifty-fifty.

Of course, married couples should share responsibilities, and one should not take advantage of the other. People in a marriage should not look for ways to suck more out of their spouse, rather, they should look for ways to be generous, sowing into their spouse. Is he all sore from work? Rub those muscles without expecting anything in return. Don't make him ask you to do it, and don't do it acting as though you really don't want to. Is she extra tired from work? Cook dinner for her (and don't make her clean it up afterward). And, don't expect a romantic night in the bedroom in return. Let the lady get some sleep.

Married couples should try to out-give one another. Don't recite a list to your spouse of all the things you do around the house and then say, *What more do you want from me?* When couples are always competing and pulling on each other for more, there will soon be nothing left to give in the marriage. This is how marriages die. Be a giver instead of a taker. Be a sower instead of a sucker.

Some wives will withhold sex from their husband unless he does certain projects around the house or lets her buy certain things that she wants. When she finally gets her way, she may think it's prosperity, but it was really prostitution. Don't milk your marriage dry, running it into the ground. Be generous to your spouse.

Chapter 9

SMALLNESS OF HEART

The leech has two daughters: Give and Give. Three things are never satisfied; four never say, "Enough".

Proverbs 30:15

The stingy soul is an unhappy soul, for it only knows a one-sided flow: you giving to me. A stingy person is like a leech, sucking the life out of everything and everyone he or she comes in contact with. The problem with stinginess is that it's never satisfied. The stingy person continually complains that they're not receiving enough, that people aren't doing enough for them. They don't understand that God has already done for them all they could ever want or need. They can't receive His provision because their heart is too narrow and small.

Stingy people come in all shapes and sizes, all ethnicities, and all economic classes. There are stingy rich people and stingy poor people. Neither are prosperous. The stingy poor person learns to function within a culture of poverty. They want everything in life on a handout basis, and think everyone owes them. They blame others for their plight and, like the leech's daughters, are always crying, *Give, give. You should do this for me, you should pay for that.* These people often live off the government, doing their part to suck the world's system dry.

Let's be clear about something: a poor person doesn't remain poor because of their circumstances or surroundings. They remain poor in life because they are poor in spirit. (A person can love God, but fail to understand the laws of His kingdom and, in the area of prosperity, be spiritually poor.) We must stop looking at poverty as an excuse and start seeing it as it is: a curse. There is no one on Earth who is destined to live a life of poverty. If a person – any person, anywhere – will look to God for His help, they can come out of poverty.

He raises up the poor from the dust; he lifts the needy from the ash heap to make them sit with princes and inherit a seat of honor.

1 Samuel 2:8

A DEPRESSION MENTALITY

It's not just poor people who are small hearted. Even when people have plenty of money, they can still be misers: steeped in stinginess. Others have what I call selective stinginess: they are generous in some areas but stingy in others. I know a great example of this kind of person: my own father.

My Dad was a great man who was loved by many people. He could be exceedingly generous to others, but was so cheap and stingy toward himself that it was humorous to watch. Having lived through the Great Depression, he carried a measure of that depression with him throughout his life. His greatest joy was to save money. If he could read without turning on a light, he would. (Why waste electricity just to read clearly?) He would wear layers of clothes before thinking to turn on the heat.

I sometimes tell the story of growing up in hot, sunny, South Florida. The air conditioning in our home, not all that efficient to begin with, broke down soon after we moved in. For some reason, Dad didn't get it fixed. For the rest of my childhood, I never again felt cool air streaming through those vents. Perhaps my Dad didn't have the money to get it repaired. I think the bigger issue was that he didn't have the will to get it repaired. He didn't care for air conditioning, which meant we didn't care for air conditioning.

We did have ceiling fans in our bedrooms. During hot evenings, we would turn on those fans so we could comfortably sleep. My Dad, however, would stay awake until my brother and I were asleep, and would then come into our room and turn off the fan. No, he didn't hate us, nor was he trying to punish us. He was just practicing his favorite hobby: saving a few cents. He could afford to run the fan, but couldn't bear the thought of it. Instead of seeing fan blades spinning, he must have visualized the electric meter spinning. We would wake up soaked in sweat because of the hot, humid air. At least Dad saved a few pennies.

My father was also obsessed with saving gasoline. He bought the most fuel efficient cars available, and would drive well out of his way to save a few cents per gallon. We spent our summers in the mountains of Northeastern Pennsylvania (no air conditioning needed there). Because the price of fuel was cheaper across the river in New Jersey, my Dad loved to go there to fuel his car. His favorite fuel-saving trick, however, was turning off the car's engine as he was driving down a hill. He knew exactly how long he could go on certain mountain roads before having to pop the clutch to re-engage the engine.

We were by no means poor growing up, but I remember things always being tight. What my Dad didn't understand was that things were tight around him because things were tight within him. Again, he didn't treat others poorly, he just had Depression-era taste.

I remember my Dad telling us about his childhood, growing up in the Depression. He would talk about how his one birthday present would be the cardboard tube from the inside of a roll of toilet paper. He would walk around blowing through that tube like it was a musical instrument. (He was a great musician. That must have been how he got started.) I can't blame him for being thrifty after having been raised with those kinds of birthday presents. It takes the gospel to change a person after growing up like that. My Dad could be a big spender, as long as it was at the flea market, garage sale, or pawn shop. I dearly love and miss my Dad. I know I mimic many of his traits, but have had to work not to replicate his thriftiness. . . I mean stinginess.

FINANCIAL PRESSURE

When people say they're being frugal, they think they're being godly, but they're often just being stingy and cheap. There's nothing godly about that. I think I understand as much as anyone what financial pressure feels like, but we must be vigilant, not allowing the pressure to constrict us on the inside. If the devil can get you small, it becomes impossible for God to enlarge you. We must not respond to pressure, we must only respond to God. If the devil sees that you respond easily to financial pressure by backing down and backing out, he will make sure that pressure never leaves you. On the other hand, there may be times when God deals with you to lighten up or tighten up. By all means obey. God's leadings are to be followed. The devil's pressure is to be ignored.

> *We are afflicted in every way, but not crushed; perplexed, but not driven to despair.*
>
> 2 Corinthians 4:8

The Greek word translated as *afflicted* means *to compress*. To compress means *to make small and narrow*. That's exactly what Satan wants to do to us, and he does it by manipulating circumstances to create pressure in our lives. The devil wants you small and narrow so you can be less of a threat to his kingdom and less effective for God.

Paul experienced this pressure first hand but said, *We are not crushed.* The Greek word translated as *crushed* means *a narrow space.* In other places, it's translated as *constricted* or *restricted.* Here's what Paul was saying: *the pressure is great on every side, but it's not making us smaller. It's not restricting or holding us back.* If the enemy couldn't make Paul smaller on the inside, he couldn't stop him. The same is true concerning us. Stay large – open-hearted – even when the pressure's on, and the enemy will not be able to keep you from moving forward. The pressure that was meant to destroy you will instead propel you.

DON'T ADAPT

I have many things written down that the Lord has spoken to me over the years. He often speaks to me in short, memorable phrases, because that's how I remember things best. I write these things down on *sticky notes* and post them on my wall so I can see them all the time. One part of my study is full of these notes. On one wall, I have this phrase written, which the Lord spoke to my heart during a time of intense financial pressure: *Don't adapt, advance.*

I'll make any changes necessary to do the will of God, but I am not to adjust to every little circumstance that comes my way. I am to seek God and follow the leadings of His Spirit. Satan desperately wants us to focus on the natural so He can constrict us, limiting our effectiveness. God, on the other hand, needs us to follow Him so He can enlarge us. Don't let the devil determine the size of your heart.

When we think of stinginess, we are quick to think of the person who slams the door in the face of the Boy Scout, or one who goes out of their way to avoid the Salvation Army volunteers as they ring their bells at Christmas time. Stinginess, however, is part of the nature of the flesh that all must overcome. Even ultra-rich people can be stingy, because they have the same flesh nature as everyone else. The temptation to hold back and yield to selfishness and stinginess escapes no one, including some of the first people who occupied the earth.

THE FIRST SCROOGE

When it was time for the harvest, Cain presented some of his crops as a gift to the Lord. Abel also brought a gift—the best of the firstborn lambs from his flock. The Lord accepted Abel and his gift, but he did not accept Cain and his gift. This made Cain very angry, and he looked dejected. "Why are you so angry?" the Lord asked Cain. "Why do you look so dejected? You will be accepted if you do what is right. But if you refuse to do what is right, then watch out! Sin is crouching at the door, eager to control you. But you must subdue it and be its master." One day Cain suggested to his brother, "Let's go out into the fields." And while they were in the field, Cain attacked his brother, Abel, and killed him.

Genesis 4:3-8 (NLT)

Of all the things I love about the Lord, one of the greatest is that he doesn't coddle us and beat around the bush. He's not wishy-washy, but is direct and, when necessary, can be quite confrontational. (People who claim that Jesus was accepting toward everyone and everything need to read the Bible.)

Two offerings were presented. One was received by the Lord and the other was not. As we have mentioned, we must not assume that an offering is received just because it was presented. Bringing the offering is just part of the equation. The more important part is how you bring it.

There were some obvious differences between Cain and Abel's offerings. Many quickly point out that Cain's was a bloodless offering, which couldn't atone for sin. That may be part of it, but there were other issues as well: heart issues. One brother did the least that he could do, while the other did the best that he could do. It wasn't just that God prefers meat to vegetables, He prefers a bountiful heart to a stingy heart. The Bible is clear as to the distinguishing feature of Abel's offering: he gave his best, and he gave *the first*:

> *Abel also brought a gift—**the best of the firstborn** lambs from his flock.*
>
> Genesis 4:4

If preachers today tried to make such a distinction between offerings, there would be disapproving frowns all over the room. Cries of legalism and manipulation would erupt, accompanied by a call for the preacher's resignation. Churches are full of people who get angry any time the preacher mentions money. Those people have the spirit of Cain, the first murderer. God, by rejecting Cain's offering, showed just how important this subject is. He wasn't just being picky, rather, He was endeavoring to fully bless His people.

Cain brought a gift, and the scriptures suggest he was the first of the brothers to do so. What was wrong with it? He yielded to the voice of his flesh that told him to bring the least instead of bringing his best. His was a stingy, low-budget offering. We shouldn't bring low-end offerings to a high-end God. Abel brought the first and he brought his best. He didn't look to find a sheep he knew he'd have a hard time selling, he looked for the choicest one of the flock. That's the kind of offering that God receives.

This is the first mention of offerings in the Bible. The first mention of any subject is important, as it establishes precedent to be followed. One thing is certain from this story: stingy offerings are unacceptable. Man may receive it, but God does not. If God doesn't receive your offering, you didn't give. If you didn't give, you won't receive. Things will get tighter. As offerings go, this was not the most successful one. The first offering coincided with the first murder.

When people hold back, they often believe they are doing so as an act of wisdom, trying to conserve money. They don't realize, however, that their act of financial wisdom is really an act of financial destruction. Squeezing harder does not increase a person, it defeats them, keeping them small on the inside. It's not circumstances that keep people small, it's their own smallness of heart.

Chapter 10

GENEROSITY

A person serving Christ must understand that everything in the world is working against them as they set out to prosper God's way. The enemy works full time to oppose prosperity, but his opposition is really an opportunity for enlargement. There will be times when it looks like none of the things of God are working for you. Be assured that they are. We need not fear opposition, yet we must be aware of it. When tests and trials come, God doesn't want you saying, *Nobody told me about this!*

The enemy works through deception, influencing the world by promoting his doctrine of smallness. News media constantly reports on shortages, price increases, etc. Their purpose is to inform, but the devil's purpose is to shrink. He wants the Body of Christ small. If he can't get them small in number, he will try to make them small in spirit. God, on the other hand, is all about enlargement, increase, and expansion. If He can get you bigger on the inside, He can make things bigger all around you. He's a big God.

*Enlarge the place of your tent, and let the curtains of your habitations be stretched out; **do not hold back**; lengthen your cords and strengthen your stakes.*

Isaiah 54:2

The only way for God to increase us is to stretch us. One of the ways he stretches us is by stretching our giving. If we want things coming back to us in large fashion, they must leave us in large fashion. Many people say they want increase but refuse to accept the stretching that precedes it. The stingy soul holds back every time the opportunity to stretch comes along. Stinginess kills prosperity.

GIVING BEYOND YOUR MEANS

*For in the midst of an ordeal of severe tribulation, their abundance of joy and their depth of poverty [together] have overflowed in wealth of **lavish generosity** on their part. For, as I can bear witness, [they gave] according to their ability, yes, and **beyond their ability**; and [they did it] voluntarily, Begging us most insistently for the favor and the fellowship of contributing in this ministration for [the relief and support of] the saints [in Jerusalem].*

2 Corinthians 8:2-4 (AMP)

Joy and poverty aren't normally found together, but for the faith person, it's a perfect mix. What do you get when you mix poverty with joy? Wealth. When poverty is responded to with faith-filled expressions of joy, the anointing flows through those expressions, turning the poverty into wealth. Does that sound fanciful or ridiculous? The same thing happened at the wedding feast of Cana, when the obedience of the servants released the anointing, turning water into wine. The key to miracles is the anointing, and it flows only where faith is found. Faith is a conductor of the anointing.

Why would anyone rejoice in the midst of lack and poverty?

Because they believe God has turned the situation around. If you want God's power to turn your situation around, you must rejoice, giving expression to your faith.

What did the churches spoken of in this passage (the churches of Macedonia) do with their new-found wealth? They gave with lavish generosity. To do something lavishly is to do it extravagantly. Extravagance isn't the normal practice of poor people, but these believers weren't poor. The poverty they were experiencing was an outward circumstance, but was nowhere to be found on the inside of them.

We have been speaking about stinginess, a deadly prosperity killer. These Macedonian believers show us the opposite of stinginess: generosity. Verse three says they gave *beyond their ability.* How do you do that? You rejoice when you feel like crying. You refuse to let the pressure constrict and constrain you on the inside. You stay big inwardly and things around you will become big.

With nothing but faith in their wallets and purses, these believers set out to give in an extravagant fashion. No evidence in the natural supported their ambitions. Any responsible person among them might have counseled them not to give the money when it came in, but rather to hold back and store up. While we are normally not to act irresponsibly, faith will often require action that looks irresponsible. For example, what would you think about a couple who was having financial difficulty, yet when a few hundred dollars came in, they agreed to use it to buy a gift card to an expensive steakhouse so their pastor could take his family out to dinner?

(Yes, I know, it's precisely this kind of rhetoric that makes the prosperity hater's skin crawl. Even many who believe in prosperity would say that this goes too far. That's fine. Stop reading if you want. Unless you want miracles. If you want miracles, keep reading.) Why would someone take the money that could buy more mac-n-cheese for their kids and purchase a luxury meal for someone who could get by without it? Faith. Faith and the prompting of the Spirit is why someone would do that.

Buying the pastor a gift card when you can't afford it sounds offensive to many, but that's essentially what the Macedonians did. They were in severe financial straits – major trouble – and when money finally comes to them, they spare no expense, giving lavishly. Although the world would call these people reckless, the Word calls them rich. One of these churches, the church at Philippi, became one of Paul's biggest supporters. You can't support ministries if you're broke. Things changed for the region of Macedonia because they didn't allow the lack that was around them to get in them. They continued to act as rich as they were.

We often hear this sage advice: *If you want to come out of financial difficulty, you must not live beyond your means.* From the natural standpoint there's much truth and wisdom there, but who wants to live only in the natural? Not the Macedonian churches. The Bible says they gave *beyond their ability*. We could say they gave beyond their means. They gave what conventional wisdom would have told them not to, and they committed to give what they did not yet have. What did their giving produce for them? A standard of living that was beyond their natural circumstances. They learned the truth that if you can give beyond your means, you can live beyond your means.

Think about how open-hearted these people must have been, giving so big when they had so little. Verse four said that the churches were begging to take part in this giving project. *Please, don't leave us out. Let us do our part. Please!* That's what begging sounds like. Begging is normally annoying, but when people are begging to give it's refreshing. It's different than when someone is pleading, *Please, give your best gift right now. Give right now or we'll have to go off the air. Please!* Preachers ought not be the ones doing the begging. The givers should be begging to give.

Maybe you've never seen an offering where people were begging to give. I have. I've been a part of spontaneous, Spirit-directed offerings, where people rushed the stage to bring their money. The minister was forced to suspend his sermon so the people, one after another, could make their way to the front to give. The piles of money on stage were so big that the ushers had to get rakes from the grounds department to gather all the money. These kinds of things shouldn't be all that unusual. When God's power is allowed to flow, great floods of finances will also flow.

There was a time during the construction of the Old Testament Tabernacle where the people were in such a flow of giving that they wouldn't stop, even after the project was fully funded. They eventually had to be physically restrained from bringing more (see Exodus 36:6). No more jewels, no more money. Keep some for the next project. The leader's job shouldn't be to try and get the people to give, their job should be to try to get them to stop when the project is fully funded. This is what generosity (the opposite of stinginess) will produce. We want this. It should be the norm, not the exception. Stinginess is a prosperity killer, but generosity is a prosperity producer.

THE LIBERAL SOUL

One gives freely, yet grows all the richer; another withholds what he should give, and only suffers want. Whoever brings blessing will be enriched, and one who waters will himself be watered.

Proverbs 11:24-25

This is a favorite passage of mine, for it encapsulates the laws of prosperity. Look at a few other translations:

*There is that scattereth, and yet increaseth; and there is that withholdeth more than is meet, but it tendeth to poverty. **The liberal soul shall be made fat**: and he that watereth shall be watered also himself. (KJV)*

Give freely and become more wealthy; be stingy and lose everything. The generous will prosper; those who refresh others will themselves be refreshed. (NLT)

This passage doesn't require much commentary. The truth is simple: give freely, grow richer. Hold back, stay in lack. Why not say that to yourself a few times: *Give freely, grow richer. Hold back, stay in lack.*

This passage shows how the laws of God's kingdom can differ from the laws of the world's kingdom. The world believes that if you give freely, you'll go broke. God, however, says that giving freely is the way to become rich. The world believes that holding tightly to what you have is the way to increase. God, on the other hand, says that's a good way to lose everything. Believers must determine which realm they desire: the kingdom of the world with all its limits, or the Kingdom of God with no limits.

Do you want to increase financially? Do you want to make progress in life, moving up to a higher standard of living? The world will tell you that it can only happen if you have certain degrees, certain contacts, or certain skills. God is much simpler. If you want to be as rich as He's made you, you can give your way there.

Again, statements like these incite the prosperity haters. They would angrily reply, *See, this is what we're talking about. You are robbing people by taking money from them, making outlandish promises that will never come to pass.* No, the person who withholds the truth from others is the one who is robbing them. I'm sorry if it sounds too good to be true. It's too good, and it is true. You can give your way to greater levels of living. The Bible makes all these amazing promises, not me. I'm just drawing attention to the teachings of Scripture.

If a person wants to grow richer, they must give freely. They must be a free-hearted, generous soul. They must not allow pressure to cause them to hold back when it's time to give. People must allow the Word to renew their minds to this truth, until they see giving as their primary occupation. What do you do for a living? I give.

If you are a thief, quit stealing. Instead, use your hands for good hard work, and then give generously to others in need.
Ephesians 4:28 (NLT)

I do work, but I work to give. How then can you live? You live off of the harvest of your giving. Stop saying, *Some of us have to work for a living, you know.* That shows that you look to your job as your source instead of looking to God. You might instead want to say that you work for a *giving.* I know of some people who worked for a giving. The great heavy equipment inventor, R.G. LeTourneau, was so committed to advancing God's kingdom that he got to the place where he was giving away ninety percent of his income and living on ten. Someone might think, *I could never live on ten percent.* If you were bringing in twenty million dollars a year, could you manage to live on the tenth? I think I could.

I know a minister, alive and still preaching today, who says that his biggest household expense every month is his giving. Plenty of money comes in every month. Everything he owns is paid for. Electric, gas, and telephone bills only cost so much. This man works for a giving and lives off his giving. He didn't start out that way, he started out in debt up to his eyeballs. He learned to give his way out and give his way to the top.

Become a giving addict. It's the greatest fun a person can have. Saying to someone, *I have this car that I'm not using, would you like it?* is one of the greatest thrills in life. Asking people, *How much do you owe on this house? How much is your car payment?* is an absolute blast. There's no greater fun than giving. Jesus certainly knew this to be the case.

> *In all things I have shown you that by working hard in this way we must help the weak and remember the words of the Lord Jesus, how he himself said, '***It is more blessed to give than to receive.***'*
>
> *Acts 20:35*

Giving and generosity are not to be minor issues for the believer, for they are not minor issues with God. If God is anything, He is a full-time giver. The central verse upon which Christians base their faith is John 3:16, which says, *God so loved the world that He gave.* Giving is everything with God, and should be everything to us. James tells us that God gives liberally, without finding fault (James 1:5). We should do the same. If we can learn to give like God gives, we can live like God lives.

There are many powerful passages that emphasize the place that giving is to have in our lives. Here's one of them:

> *And God is able to make all grace abound to you, so that having all sufficiency in all things at all times, you may abound in every good work. As it is written, "He has distributed freely, he has given to the poor; his righteousness endures forever." He who supplies seed to the sower and bread for food will supply and multiply your seed for sowing and increase the harvest of your righteousness. You will be enriched in every way to be generous in every way, which through us will pro-*

duce thanksgiving to God.

2 Corinthians 9:8-11

There is so much in this passage that we could speak of. For now, however, notice the part of the last verse which says we will be *enriched in every way so we can be generous in every way. Enriched* means *made rich.* We are rich in every way. We are generous on every occasion. We abound to every good work. It would help to speak these things over yourself regularly. Say, *I am rich in every way. I am generous in every way. I give into every good work.* Thank God it's true!

Chapter 11

DRENCHED

Whoever brings blessing will be enriched, and one who waters will himself be watered.

Proverbs 11:25

This verse is an example of the power of the law of sowing and reaping (or, giving and receiving). We'll speak about this law in more detail later, but notice that if you want something to happen for you, you should first seek to make it happen for someone else. It's sowing and reaping, not reaping and sowing. If you bring blessing to someone else, you will end up being blessed.

This verse speaks of *watering* someone. What exactly does that mean? I began to study this verse and discovered that the Hebrew word translated as *water* literally means *to drench*. When I read that, I was reminded of an experience I had a few years back.

Although I have time for very few hobbies, I do enjoy riding my motorcycle. Getting away for a little bit seems to help me unwind, and God often ministers to me as I am riding along, fellowshipping with Him. We had recently moved across the country and it had been a long time since I had been able to get away for a ride. On this particular day, I needed to go look at something at a store about an hour away. The sky was blue and it seemed like the perfect day to jump on the bike and take care of business at the same time.

I was planning to leave for this short trip right after lunch. My wife advised me to check the weather before I left, so, like a good husband, I heeded her advice and pulled up the radar map on my computer. Everything looked clear, so I closed the computer and headed outside.

What I didn't realize was that the radar map on the computer has different layers. First, the map of the area comes up, and then the radar loads as a separate layer of graphics. I saw the map and thought all was clear, but had never waited for the radar to appear. I enjoyed my ride down to the store and took care of my business. When I came out of the store to ride home, however, it looked like Armageddon was about to take place in the sky. I thought perhaps I could get ahead of the storm, so I hustled on my way. I had been riding for about ten minutes when the heavens broke loose.

Because we had just moved, my motorcycle gear, including my rain suit, was still packed away in a box. I'm sharing this story to illustrate that I fully understand the meaning of the word *drenched*. To say that I got soaked would be inaccurate. There was not a part of my body unaffected by that storm. I was completely water-logged. I had my tall leather riding boots on, but it didn't matter. Water had found its way everywhere.

When a person is drenched with the blessing of the Lord, every area of his or her life is affected. Nothing is excluded. That's what I want: His blessing on every part of my life; no area kept back from His touch. If you want your life to be drenched, believe God to help drench someone else's life. I have been a part of some offerings where several people got together and absolutely drenched someone. We blessed the person with an over-the-top offering. We need more of these drench-offerings. Any time you have the opportunity to drench someone, do it. If you will water them, you will be watered yourself.

WATERED

Some versions of the Bible translate *watered* as *refreshed*. That helps our understanding some, yet the Hebrew word really is *watered*. What does it mean to water someone? I initially thought about when Jesus spoke of giving someone a cup of cold water. That would certainly be a refreshing gesture, but I wondered if there was an even better scriptural example. There is, and it's found in the story of Abraham's servant, when he went to find a wife for Abraham's son, Isaac.

> *Then the servant took ten of his master's camels and departed, taking all sorts of choice gifts from his master; and he arose and went to Mesopotamia to the city of Nahor. And he made the camels kneel down outside the city by the well of water at the time of evening, the time when women go out to draw water. And he said, "O Lord, God of my master Abraham, please grant me success today and show steadfast love to my master Abraham. Behold, I am standing by the spring of water, and the daughters of the men of the city are coming out to draw water. Let the young woman to whom I shall say, 'Please let down your jar that I may drink,' and who shall say, 'Drink, and I will water your camels'—let her be the one whom you*

have appointed for your servant Isaac. By this I shall know that you have shown steadfast love to my master."

Genesis 24:10-14

Why would Abraham's servant ask such a thing of the Lord? Was he just too lazy to water the camels himself? No, he needed to find someone who wouldn't stop the flow of prosperity that was in his master's house, but would instead help perpetuate it. He needed to find someone with a heart big enough to receive and properly handle enormous amounts of wealth and blessing. That meant he needed to find someone who's heart was wide open to give, who would go above and beyond his request, spontaneously demonstrating a heart of generosity without even a thought of self. He found her. Her name was Rebekah.

Before he had finished speaking, behold, Rebekah, who was born to Bethuel the son of Milcah, the wife of Nahor, Abraham's brother, came out with her water jar on her shoulder. The young woman was very attractive in appearance, a maiden whom no man had known. She went down to the spring and filled her jar and came up. Then the servant ran to meet her and said, "Please give me a little water to drink from your jar." She said, "Drink, my lord." And she quickly let down her jar upon her hand and gave him a drink. When she had finished giving him a drink, she said, "I will draw water for your camels also, until they have finished drinking." So she quickly emptied her jar into the trough and ran again to the well to draw water, and she drew for all his camels.

Genesis 24:15-20

This is more amazing than many have thought. She said, *I will*

draw water for your camels also, until they have finished drinking.
These ten camels were at the end of their journey. A thirsty cam-
el can drink up to forty gallons of water when he finally stops to
drink. Rebekeh had a water pot on her shoulder that couldn't
have held more than two or three gallons. She had to be able to
easily pick it up and set it down.

She drew up to four hundred gallons of water for these ten
thirsty camels. How many trips is that? Well over a hundred
times, dipping the jar in and pouring it out. This was not just
a short five minute delay. Back home, her mom was probably
waiting for her to bring the water so she could boil the spaghetti noodles for dinner, but Rebekah didn't return. Watering all
those camels was hard physical labor.

What Rebekah didn't know is that those camels were laden
with jewelry and other valuable gifts that represented but a portion of what would be her's back at Abraham's house. She watered those camels and got watered herself. She drenched Abraham's servant and got drenched herself. No part of her life would
escape the blessing that was now hers.

Do you want your life overflowing with precious things? Develop a heart of generosity. Resist stinginess. Look for opportunities to be a blessing to others. And, when the Lord deals with
you to do something for someone, do it to the max. Drench
them, and you'll be drenched.

Learn to be a liberal soul. Practice generosity by operating at
a level where you can be free-hearted. Take someone out to dinner and pay for their meal. Don't allow yourself to have a sepa-

rate-checks mentality any longer. Do what you can do generous-ly. It's better to be a big spender at a fast food restaurant than to be a miser at a steakhouse. You may start out by paying for one person's meal, but feed on the scriptures in these chapters until you can see yourself paying for a whole group of people. Be generous at your current income level and it won't be long until you find yourself at a higher level.

PROSPERITY PREACHERS: MY INSIDE VIEW

There's one more thing I'd like to address while speaking about the prosperity killer called stinginess, and it's much-preferred opposite, generosity.

Over the years, I have been blessed to be around many ministers. Being on staff at one of the largest Charismatic ministries in the world, I met and observed some of the most well-known ministers of the day, including ones that prosperity haters write books about. I've been backstage with them and have sat at the table with them for meals, listening to them talk. In a few cases, I have worked closely with them, spending time in their palatial homes and flying on their private jets.

From time to time, I stumble upon one of the many internet articles trashing prosperity preachers: calling them by name, criticizing their possessions, and warning the rest of the Body of Christ to beware of their deceptions. While reading, I often think to myself, *I know these people personally.* (I don't mean that I have close relationships with them. I just mean I've spent time around them.) I guess you could say that I'm a prosperity insider.

I would like to provide a first-hand account of the actions of these people: the ones our opponents call *prosperity pimps*. Here, in one brief statement, are the behind-the-scenes secrets of the prosperity movement:

> *These prosperity preachers are the most generous, humble, selfless people I have ever been around.*

I want to be just like them. I have seen them empty their bank accounts to help meet needs in the Body of Christ. I've seen them expend great effort to be a blessing, without even receiving a *thank you* in return. I have watched them silently do things for people that would make most Christians weep. They are not the hard-hearted greed-mongers that our critics make them out to be. I've never seen an ounce of greed in them. Compared to God, money means nothing to these people. They have plenty of it, not because they are materialistic, but because they understand how to flow with the laws of the Kingdom of God.

Before believing everything you read in books or on the internet, look at the fruit in a person's life. If there's something you don't understand, or that concerns you, just leave it in God's hands. Sure, there have been those who have abused the message of prosperity. I'm not denying that. However, those individuals are not the people I am speaking of. I've been blessed to be around honorable people, not those who abuse others. Anyone who abuses others and appears to be prosperous won't have their prosperity for long. The ones who prosper and flourish for the long term gave their way there, guaranteed. It's just not possible to prosper while yielding to the prosperity killers.

Chapter 12

STRIFE

We have spoken about stinginess (smallness of heart), and generosity, a largeness of heart. The generous soul has a wide-open, free spirit that is open to give anything God directs. Keeping our heart right at all times is essential to prosperity. Let's look at an interesting passage, spoken by Jesus:

> *You have heard that it was said, An eye for an eye and a tooth for a tooth. But I say to you, Do not resist the one who is evil. But if anyone slaps you on the right cheek, turn to him the other also. And if anyone would sue you and take your tunic, let him have your cloak as well. And if anyone forces you to go one mile, go with him two miles. Give to the one who begs from you, and do not refuse the one who would borrow from you.*
>
> *Matthew 5:38-42*

Eloquent words spoken by the Master, but is this the same Jesus who, a few chapters later, was whipping people in the temple? Why the sudden display of pacifism? Why would he allow us to be taken advantage of in such a way? He's not. The only way someone can take advantage of you is if they can get you to shrivel up and hold back on the inside. Jesus spoke these words to protect us from smallness of heart.

What's the natural thing to do when someone slaps you? Slap them right back, even harder. What if someone takes something from you? You want to take from them, spitefully drawing every blessing out of their life (like the leech). If we allow ourselves to respond in kind when presented with an offense, we close our heart. If our heart is closed, we cannot receive from God.

The reason we turn our cheek, or give our cloak when someone takes our tunic, is to keep our heart open. If we don't purposely take action to keep our heart open, it will close up during times of stress and conflict. It's for this reason that we must avoid fighting with others: it closes up our heart and keeps us from receiving. Truly, there's no quicker way to kill your prosperity than to yield to strife. Strife is a prosperity killer.

People going through a divorce must be careful in this area. Divorce often kills the prosperity of both parties, but it's not the dividing of assets that brings poverty as much as the narrowness of heart and all the fighting, pulling, and taking.

NO STRIFE

One of the most powerful lessons in the scriptures concerning strife is found in Genesis: the first book of the Bible.

*And Lot, who went with Abram, also had flocks and herds and tents, so that the land could not support both of them dwelling together; for their possessions were so great that they could not dwell together, and **there was strife** between the herdsmen of Abram's livestock and the herdsmen of Lot's livestock. At that time the Canaanites and the Perizzites were* *dwelling in the land. Then Abram said to Lot, "**Let there be no strife** between you and me, and between your herdsmen and my herdsmen, for we are kinsmen. Is not the whole land before you? Separate yourself from me. If you take the left hand, then I will go to the right, or if you take the right hand, then I will go to the left."*

Genesis 13:5-9

God had blessed Abraham exceedingly. Verse 2 of Genesis 13 says, *Now Abram was very rich in livestock, in silver, and in gold.* When God brings His blessing into your life, especially to the degree that Abraham had experienced, you know how it came about. Abraham knew that God was the one who had made him rich. He also understood that certain things would hinder his prosperity if allowed to remain in his life. When strife rose up in his camp, Abraham swiftly rose up to deal with it.

Abraham said, *Let there be no strife.* No strife. That's not the standard that most Christians hold to. Most are okay with at least some strife.

Is this really such a big deal? You bet it is. If it wasn't, Abraham wouldn't have sent his closest relative packing, forcing him to find somewhere else to live. Believers think it's normal to argue, fuss, fight, bicker, lie, hold grudges, and offer the silent treatment. They think that's just what family does, but they are deceived, believing that none of it affects their prosperity. Strife kills prosperity. Satan loves it when Christians fight other people.

Abraham didn't say, *Let there be less strife between us.* He said *no strife*. He would have none of it. If you want God's prosperity, you must adopt Abraham's attitude toward strife: if you're going to fight, you're out.

For the believer, the opposite of strife is walking in love. We understand from the scriptures that love is to be our chief occupation. The New Testament clearly exalts love as the highest quality of heart and action that the believer is to embrace. For the same reason that love is exalted, strife is forbidden. God cannot bless strife. It's a blessing killer, a prosperity killer.

Abraham told Lot to leave, giving him the pick of the land. The astounding thing is that Lot actually left.

Prosperity opponents use this passage as an example of why it's wrong to have anything besides life's most basic possessions. *Money causes problems*, they often say. No, a lack of money causes problems. Only when there's money without character are there problems. Lot didn't have cattle issues, he had character issues.

Lot should never have been comfortable with the thought of leaving his uncle and going out on his own. He should have realized that the only reason he was so blessed was that he was partaking of Abraham's blessing. His desire for riches caused him to fall into temptation and a snare, plunging him into destruction (1 Timothy 6:9). People (like Lot) who serve others often partake of the anointing and blessing on the lives of those they serve. We must be careful not to mistake the blessing on our leader's life as our own.

When I was traveling with Brother Hagin, I was mightily

blessed. I was regularly on stage in front of thousands of people. Ministers all over the country knew me and some began having me in their churches to minister in music and the Word. After many years, I felt led to leave Brother Hagin's ministry to go start a church. I instantly found out what it was like to be out from under his anointing. The crowds didn't follow me, they stayed with him. I realized that the anointing I had been enjoying really wasn't mine, but his. Once out on my own, I felt spiritually naked. After I left, I continued traveling to his meetings whenever I could. I wanted to be back under his anointing until mine could develop.

Lot should never have left Abraham without begging him to reconsider, but I'm not sure staying with Abraham even crossed Lot's mind. He seemed all too eager to comply and depart. He must have thought, *Abraham has been holding me back all these years with his rules and restrictions. He's just jealous of all my cattle. Once I'm out on my own and can be "the man" things will be better.*

People in ministry and business often say these same kinds of things about their leaders. Even worse, they leave, just like Lot. Once Lot left and moved to Sodom, we never again hear of his cattle. He ended up losing the very thing that he couldn't bring himself to release. Eventually he lost everything. Lot's prosperity had never really been his own, but was the result of his association with Abraham. If we repeat Lot's error, we will have Lot's results.

Lot further displayed poor character by choosing the best part of the land. When Abraham insisted on his departure, Lot should have said, *Uncle Abraham, if I have to go, you choose the best land and I'll take what's left.* Lot instead chose the best for himself, leaving Abraham with the leftovers. How did things work out for Abraham? Did he suffer, having been left with the poor part of the land? Hardly. We see that once strife was removed, the flow of God was restored and great prosperity was the result.

> *The Lord said to Abram, after Lot had separated from him, "Lift up your eyes and look from the place where you are, northward and southward and eastward and westward, for all the land that you see I will give to you and to your off- spring forever. I will make your offspring as the dust of the earth, so that if one can count the dust of the earth, your off- spring also can be counted. Arise, walk through the length and the breadth of the land, for I will give it to you."*
>
> *Genesis 13:14-17*

Pay whatever it costs to get rid of strife now, or you'll pay everything later. Abraham understood this. I know people who have paid large sums of money to settle disputes with people who were constant sources of strife and friction. They weren't in the wrong, yet they knew they couldn't afford to allow strife to remain.

STRIFE IN THE HOME

> *It is better to dwell in a corner of the housetop, than with a brawling woman in a wide house.*
>
> *Proverbs 21:9 (KJV)*

The Hebrew word translated as *brawling* indicates *a quarrel that cannot be stopped once it starts*. There are some people who are chronic fighters and will never stop. Do not marry strife. Do not date strife. Stay away from strife.

Think about two people who may have married each other for money. They are like the leech's daughters, squeezing the life out of their marriage and fighting all the time. They may have started out in a big house, but because their character is poor and they regularly yield to strife, they will someday end up losing their big house. They cannot maintain prosperity on the outside, because they are not prosperous on the inside.

Now think about another couple, a peace-loving, God-loving couple. They marry with little more than their love for each other and their love for God, therefore they can only afford to rent an attic apartment (the *corner of the housetop*). This couple has committed to not allow strife in their home. Because they won't yield to the prosperity killers, God can increase and prosper this couple, who might someday end up owning the first couple's house after they lose it.

The beginning of strife is like letting out water, so quit before the quarrel breaks out.

Proverbs 17:14

The start of a quarrel is like a leak in a dam, so stop it before it bursts. (MSG)

Every couple contemplating marriage should be required to

learn this verse. You work hard, sow seed, and believe God in order to have your life filled with His blessings. Then, one good argument causes it all to start leaking out. I sometimes think of the old fashioned stoppers that we used to use in sinks and tubs. Once you pulled the stopper, the water began to drain. If you didn't replace the stopper, there would be no water left. Don't spend years filling up your tub of blessing, then allow strife to pull the plug. While you're thinking of the next thing to say in your argument, your prosperity is spiraling down the drain.

I heard a minister tell about an experience that she had along these lines. She and her husband had been in strife: not a knock-down, drag-out kind of fight, but more like an extended feud. During this time, their newborn child had to go to the emergency room. Their health insurance didn't cover this particular visit so they had to pay a hospital bill totalling several thousand dollars. It was a hard lesson to learn, but the Lord showed this couple that their strife had allowed God's blessing to drain out, so to speak, allowing the enemy to afflict their child. Strife also drained their bank account. Let's learn from their lesson, avoiding the consequences they had to endure.

WALKING IN LOVE

Love does no wrong to one's neighbor [it never hurts anybody]. Therefore love meets all the requirements and is the fulfilling of the Law.

Romans 13:10 (AMP)

If a person refuses to walk in love (treating others right). they will kill their prosperity. You cannot use your mouth against other people and expect to prosper. People must understand that when they lean in to gossip about someone, they are really saying, *Goodbye blessings, you can't come any closer.* Christians commit these errors every day. Then they cry about their financial difficulties, saying, *I don't understand. I dispatched the angels to bring the money in like the preacher talked about.* Yes, and when you gossiped you also dispatched the devils to steal from you. Many people kill their prosperity with their mouth.

You cannot be jealous of the blessings of others and expect to prosper. You cannot allow yourself to be eaten up with envy. These things are evil and have no place in the believer who wants to prosper.

For where envying and strife is, there is confusion and every evil work.

James 3:16 (KJV)

The opposite of strife is peace. Peace is like a magnet, drawing in the prosperity of God. Prosperity only lands where peace is found. God can work where there's peace, because His peace is a manifestation of His presence. Conversely, strife is a manifestation of the devil's presence, opening the door for him to steal, kill, and destroy.

Chapter 13

UNFAITHFULNESS

One who is faithful in a very little is also faithful in much, and one who is dishonest in a very little is also dishonest in much. If then you have not been faithful in the unrighteous wealth, who will entrust to you the true riches? And if you have not been faithful in that which is another's, who will give you that which is your own? No servant can serve two masters, for either he will hate the one and love the other, or he will be devoted to the one and despise the other. You cannot serve God and money.

Luke 16:10-13

LITTLE THINGS

The problem with little things is that people think they are little things. God, on the other hand, is clear that little things are the biggest thing when determining our prosperity. Little things determine how big we get.

Many have the erroneous idea that when things are small, they don't matter much, but when they grow big they suddenly become more important. They think, *I know I'm fudging it now, but I'll do it right when we grow.* According the the Word of God, that's not true. You will do then what you are doing now, just a larger version of it. God does not promote to greater levels of responsibility and increase until a person passes tests of faithfulness.

God looks at how we handle things when they are *very little*. That's talking about day one. Whether we're speaking of business, ministry, or a large corporation, faithfulness and honesty are required. This passage mentions being honest with very little. When things are small, we are tempted to think that dishonesty will go undetected by others. Society has taught us that small amounts of carefully placed dishonesty, slipped in here and there, are acceptable: that it's okay to tell little white lies. God disagrees. He knows that what you do when things are small is what you'll do when they get bigger.

We've all heard the unfortunate stories of those who were victims of Ponzi schemes (when an investment broker robs from certain clients in order to help grow his fund or pay other clients). By the time the broker gets caught, billions of dollars are gone. I guarantee that no broker ever set out intending to rob billions from his clients. It began when things were small and he said, *I wouldn't do this if it were a larger amount, but it will be okay just this one time*. Little things are such a big deal because little things turn into big things.

Have you ever gone into the supply closet at work to get some things for your desk, and slipped a few of those pens in your pocket to take home? People think, *It's just pens*, or, *it's just paperclips*. No, it's your prosperity. You're killing it. Even more dangerous is the kind of thinking that says, *Well, if they paid me more, I wouldn't have to take these things.* They pay you what you agreed to work for. Stop being a leech and get back to work. Be faithful in the little things and treat them like big things.

People who excel in life are ones who give attention to detail. In the world of business and commerce, people have learned how important little things can be. Coffee shops know that it's not enough just to use quality coffee beans. Quality must be evident in every area, at every location, and it must be that way every day. The creamers and flavors must be outstanding, the seating areas must be comfortable, and even the cups must have an attractive design. Entire brands are built on quality, which means that someone is paying attention to little things. The Church should possess at least as much diligence and excellence as a coffee shop.

The way you handle the resources you currently have determines whether you will be entrusted with more. For example, many believers would like to purchase their own house, or a better house. They pray and might sow some seed, but those are not the only requirements for enlargement. Faithfulness must also be evident. How the believer treats their current home is one of the biggest factors in determining whether they will ever qualify for greater.

If you are believing God for a dream home, but your current home is a nightmare, I have news for you: there's no dream home coming. I've been in the homes of believers where things are broken, paint is peeling, the garage is a mess, piles of stuff are everywhere, and everything is dirty and disorganized. Some of these same homeowners are believing that God will upgrade them. They talk about, *When I get my new place. . . .* There is no new place, until you make your current place look like your new place.

Many find this kind of teaching tiresome, complaining, *Come on, these are just little things.* That's right, they are, but little things are everything with God. Little things are prosperity qualifiers and prosperity killers.

TRUE RICHES

Notice that verse 11 says, *If then you have not been faithful in the unrighteous wealth, who will entrust to you the true riches?* The phrase *unrighteous wealth* is not meant to indicate that money is evil. It could be better translated this way: *the wealth that the unrighteous use and possess.* This is referring to the trading currencies of our world system. What's clear is this: if we are not faithful with money, we will not be entrusted with what Jesus called *true riches.*

What does the Bible mean by *true riches?* It must be referring to a substance with more value than money, a substance with which man could be entrusted. One substance that satisfies that description is the anointing. The anointing is God's power: His presence, His glory, His increase. These things would certainly qualify as true riches.

How does God determine whether a person qualifies for true riches? He looks at how they handle money and earthly things. Those who say money and material possessions don't matter are forgetting this verse. They matter greatly. According to this passage, our stewardship in the area of finances is the first place God looks to evaluate our faithfulness. He is in need of more people to whom He can entrust both natural and spiritual (true) riches. May He look at us and find that we qualify. We know that it's not appropriate to lust after material riches, but we are permitted to set our affection on true riches. I want all of His anointing that I can get!

OTHER PEOPLE'S THINGS

And if you have not been faithful in that which is another's, who will give you that which is your own?

Luke 16:12

According to the Bible, the way you treat someone else's possessions determines if and when you will receive your own. God allows us to prove our faithfulness using someone else's equipment, handling someone else's money, serving in someone else's ministry, etc. People everywhere want to be in charge and be their own boss. They're tired of working for the other man. That's fine, if that's what God wants for you, but let's ask a few questions first to see if you qualify.

Do you show up on time, all the time, or are you routinely late? Do you talk poorly about the boss when he or she is not around? Do you gather contact information of clients at work so that you can solicit their business when you go out on your own? Do you spend your boss's money more liberally than you should, wasting your company's resources? If any of these things are taking place, they will have to change before God will promote you to a business of your own.

PROVING MY FAITHFULNESS

I work in my own ministry today, but I'm glad that the Lord allowed me to spend years serving and working for other people. I had to learn to treat their resources as carefully as I would treat my own.

I am reminded of one instance that occurred while I was working for a large ministry. I was in charge of producing recording projects for this ministry and had a very generous budget with which to work. I was accountable for the funds with which I was entrusted, however, I was really the only one who knew all the financial details of the project. Looking back, I see that it would have been easy to channel some of the money my way, although that thought never crossed my mind at the time.

I spent an enormous amount of time working on one particular project. During a several month period, I probably worked twice the amount of hours for which I was being paid. I did most of the work myself, and contracted others to help me with the rest. One of the producers I had hired fell behind on his work, and was in danger of holding up the completion of the project. After communicating with him, I jumped in to lighten his workload. That got the project back on track.

After the project was complete and all the bills were paid, I received a large check from this person. He said that since I had done about half of his work, he felt it was only right to pay me accordingly.

This man was endeavoring to be honorable and do the right thing. Although it was right for him to pay me for picking up his slack, it wasn't necessarily right for me to receive it. Why? Because those funds originally came from the ministry I was working for. For me to have the ministry pay him, and then receive a portion of those funds back without the ministry's knowledge, is what's known as a *kickback*. Kickbacks, unless disclosed, are unethical, and often illegal.

I didn't know exactly how this should be handled. That's because it wasn't my place to know. I had been entrusted to make almost every decision related to this project, however, this one wasn't mine to make. This decision belonged to those over me. I wrote a short letter to my boss's secretary explaining what had happened and attached the check to it. A few days later, I received a correspondence back, along with the check, telling me to keep it for a job well done.

This was much more than just a business transaction, it was a test of my faithfulness: a test of my heart. It seemed almost certain that no one would have known had I just cashed the check and kept the money. Perhaps they wouldn't have found out, but God knew. I could have kept the money, but would have killed my prosperity. I believe that one of the reasons why God has been able to bring large sums into our ministry at times is because I demonstrated faithfulness when the funds weren't mine.

FAITHFULNESS IN MINISTRY

Ministers who receive offerings must pass these same kinds of tests. Even if the ministry has your name on it, the ministry is not really yours; it belongs to God. He requires faithful stewardship over the resources He brings your way.

Moreover, it is required of stewards that they be found faithful.

1 Corinthians 4:2

Be faithful when the ministry is small or just starting out. When the offerings are small, treat them with as much care and importance as you would if they were large and substantial. Learn enough about accounting to be able to know if the books are being kept correctly. Exercise good stewardship over your facility, even if it's not yours.

There was a period of time when our church met in a rented facility that was used by others during the week. We would just come in on Sunday morning and have our service. Before the people arrived, I would walk through the bathrooms to make sure they were clean; I knew the cleaning staff at this facility had low standards of excellence. After an event on Saturday evening, there might be empty beer bottles all over the place that needed to be discarded. Although someone else was being paid to take care of these things, I still considered it my responsibility. We always left our facility neater and cleaner than we found it.

For ten of the eleven years that I pastored, we had our own rented facility. That building didn't belong to us, yet we made many improvements over the years at our own expense. When we moved out, our landlord was left with new bathrooms, new furnaces, new carpet, etc., all of which we had paid for. Even though we knew we couldn't take those things with us, we considered them worthwhile expenses: whatever it takes to help advance God's kingdom. Whatever it takes to be counted faithful.

Chapter 14

STEWARDSHIP

Jesus spent much time describing the Kingdom of God – a new system of government – and its laws. His words were recorded for our benefit, that we might align ourselves with His kingdom and experience His increase. Below, we see the story of a man who went away on a long trip, commissioning his servants to faithfully manage his assets. Jesus narrates the story, as the man returns and receives an accounting from his servants.

*Now after a long time the master of those servants came and settled accounts with them. And he who had received the five talents came forward, bringing five talents more, saying, 'Master, you delivered to me five talents; here I have made five talents more.' His master said to him, 'Well done, **good and faithful servant**. You have been faithful over a little; I will set you over much. Enter into the joy of your master.' And he also who had the two talents came forward, saying, 'Master, you delivered to me two talents; here I have made two talents more.' His master said to him, 'Well done, good and faithful servant. You have been faithful over a little; I will set you over much. Enter into the joy of your master.' He also who had received the one talent came forward, saying, 'Master, I knew you to be a hard man, reaping where you did not sow, and gathering where you scattered no seed, so I was afraid, and I went and hid your talent in the ground. Here you have what is yours.' But his master answered him, 'You wicked and* *slothful servant! You knew that I reap where I have not sown and gather where I scattered no seed? Then you ought to have invested my money with the bankers, and at my coming I should have received what was my own with interest. So take the talent from him and give it to him who has the ten talents. **For to everyone who has will more be given, and he will have an abundance. But from the one who has not, even what he has will be taken away.** And cast the worthless servant into the outer darkness. In that place there will be weeping and gnashing of teeth.'*

Matthew 25:19-30

Notice the emphasis here on faithfulness. The master didn't say *good and talented servant* or *good and anointed servant*, it was their faithfulness that brought promotion. What had they been faithful to do? They faithfully took what they had been entrusted with and caused it to grow.

As we serve others, proving our faithfulness, we should bring increase to our place of service. If you work for a company or corporation, that corporation should be increasing because of you. You should bring more than just your natural skill to your place of service; you should also bring your faith. No matter how insignificant your position, faithfulness will bring promotion and unfaithfulness will bring disqualification. Never look at the smallness of your situation and become discouraged. Every large tree began as a small seed. In the Kingdom of God, everything begins small.

Two of the servants brought increase to their master and were counted faithful. The third brought no increase and was called wicked and slothful. (Isn't it interesting that Jesus equates poor stewardship to wickedness?) This servant did nothing to multiply his master's resources; he considered the assets in his care too insignificant to matter. He failed to esteem the laws of the kingdom, and failed to appreciate the value of little things. We can see why the master didn't give him much to begin with.

THE HAVES AND THE HAVE NOTS

Jesus' statement in verse 29 shows that faithfulness is a prosperity multiplier, and unfaithfulness a prosperity killer:

For to everyone who has will more be given, and he will have an abundance. But from the one who has not, even what he has will be taken away.

This statement is in stark contrast to the views of many who think that forcing an even distribution of wealth is the key to prosperity. Many have a Robin Hood mentality that believes that the increase of the poor requires the depletion of the rich. People are often prejudiced against the rich, assuming that they became rich by taking advantage of the poor. By no means is that always the case. Isn't it possible for the rich person to become rich, not by taking advantage of the poor, but by taking advantage of the laws of the Kingdom of God?

Jesus tells us the truth about the *haves* and the *have nots*. The one who has will have more, and the one who has not will lose what he has. What is it that these people have or don't have? An understanding of the laws of prosperity, and the faithfulness to keep those laws working long term. A person can have nothing in terms of possessions but still *have* – possessing an understanding of the laws of God – and begin to increase and enjoy abundance. Others may be loaded with possessions but still *have not* – not understanding how God works – and end up losing all. Don't believe it? Just look around. This happens all the time.

People, every day, kill their prosperity by violating God's laws, and then blame the rich for their problems. Had Jesus told this story in our day, it would have enraged His audience. Think about it: the master in this story actually took all that the poorest servant had and gave it to the richest. Politicians in our day would condemn Jesus for this kind of teaching. News outlets would have a heyday; there would be no end to the headlines. Society may think it unfair, political leaders may call it wrong, but the truth remains: in the Kingdom of God, those who are blessed often continue to increase, while others go from bad to worse. (It should again be stated: the Bible teaches care for the poor, promising blessing to those who reach out to the less fortunate. That care, however, is not how the poor are to perpetually live.)

THE WEALTH OF THE SINNER

Are there other scriptures that teach about the *haves* and the *have nots* (those who increase and those who fail to increase)? Indeed there are.

A good man leaves an inheritance to his children's children, but the sinner's wealth is laid up for the righteous.

Proverbs 13:22

Prosperity-believers love this scripture, but often have a fuzzy idea of how it might come to pass. The reality is, for most people, it won't come to pass; they don't qualify. People have long taught of an end-time transfer of the world's wealth into the Church. There is certainly truth to that thought, but many believe this transfer is something that God will suddenly make happen on His own, the money just somehow showing up so we can get to work. If that's your belief, you believe incorrectly.

First of all, large sums of money won't come to the Church in order to make the Church prosperous, those sums would only come if the Church already were prosperous (which, sadly, is often not the case). If great sums suddenly did appear, most in the Church would soon be broke again. When people are not inwardly prosperous, outward prosperity is only a temporary condition. Such believers would soon lose the money that had come into their hands. Unfaithfulness and poor stewardship is a big reason why an end-time transfer of wealth won't happen for most people.

We must understand that money, by itself, does not indicate prosperity. Prosperity is a heart condition more than a financial condition. People who run drug, gambling, and prostitution rings have money, but they are not prosperous in any sense of the word. Most in the Body of Christ are not prosperous inwardly, and therefore cannot truly prosper in life. More money would just magnify the prosperity killers at work within them, making their downfall more dramatic. It's actually God's mercy that some people have so little.

It's been said that the smallest percentage of the population controls most of the wealth in our world. If that money was evenly distributed throughout the population of the planet, it would not be long until that same small percentage of people again controlled most of the wealth. The ones who have learned how to prosper will be the ones who will prosper.

In what way then, is the sinner's wealth laid up for the righteous? The righteous person (not just the saved person, but the one who walks in the light of his or her righteousness) understands the laws of the kingdom and knows how to prosper by working those laws. We don't have to steal from the sinner to get their wealth, we need only cooperate with the laws of the kingdom. We need only avoid the prosperity killers. There is indeed the need for great sums of the world's wealth to fund the work of God in the Earth. God can deal with the sinner if need be to help fund His works, but would prefer to be able to direct His own children.

> *For to the person who pleases Him God gives wisdom and knowledge and joy; but to the sinner He gives the work of gathering and heaping up, that he may give to one who pleases God. This also is vanity and a striving after the wind and a feeding on it.*
>
> *Ecclesiastes 2:26 (AMP)*

Again, the person who thinks that this kind of wealth transfer happens automatically is in need of greater revelation. Just being in the family of God does not mean a person is qualified for increase. It's true that, for the sinner, all their toil is emptiness and vanity. God indeed has the sinner working – gathering and heaping up – that He may channel those resources into the hands of those who are faithful, understanding how to cooperate with God.

Here's yet another verse that shows the deceitfulness of riches, the emptiness of the lives of those that set their heart on them, and God's greater plans for the money to which they are clinging.

> Go to now, ye rich men, weep and howl for your miseries that shall come upon you. Your riches are corrupted, and your garments are motheaten. Your gold and silver is cankered; and the rust of them shall be a witness against you, and shall eat your flesh as it were fire. **Ye have heaped treasure together for the last days.**
>
> James 5:1-3 (KJV)

The sinner thinks that they are heaping treasure together for *their* last days, but the Bible indicates that they're storing up treasure for *the* last days. There is wealth that belongs in the hands of the people of God. I'm convinced that one reason why we haven't seen more of it come in is that many in the Body of Christ have disqualified themselves through unfaithfulness. It's time to learn God's ways and accomplish His works.

GRADUAL INCREASE

*Whoever works his land will have plenty of bread, but he who follows worthless pursuits will have plenty of poverty. **A faithful man will abound with blessings**, but whoever hastens to be rich will not go unpunished.*

Proverbs 28:19-20

A consistent theme in Scripture is that the believer progresses to different levels of increase gradually, rather than suddenly. Many are looking off in the distance, waiting for a spectacular prosperity event to occur. God can and does do wonderful things that may even seem sudden, yet we are not to think of sudden events as our normal flow of prosperity. The Bible emphasizes faithfulness as the key to blessing, rather than trying to get something to happen instantly. You're going to have to *work your land* every day if you want to abound.

Faithfulness requires daily discipline. When needs present themselves, people decide, *I need to make something happen now*. They get overly excited about their new home-based business, or an investment that promises unrealistic returns, not realizing that in many cases they are following what the Bible calls *worthless pursuits*. If God leads a person to a business or investment, fine, but hastening and scrambling after money is no substitute for faithfulness over the long term. Prosperity is not a one-time event, it's a lifetime commitment. I plan to be faithful, and because God is faithful, I know that I will *abound with blessings*.

Chapter 15

THE PATH

For I know the plans I have for you, declares the Lord, plans to prosper you and not to harm you, plans to give you hope and a future.

Jeremiah 29:11 (NIV)

This is one of the most beloved and well known verses among Christians, and for good reason: it's true! Many, however, have adopted an unscriptural interpretation of it. It's easy to read this verse and think, *God has plans to prosper me, therefore I'll prosper.* That's not true! Just because God plans or desires something for you doesn't mean you'll ever experience it. We must follow His plans in order to enjoy His prosperity. Prosperity isn't something that happens *to* you, it's something that happens *with* you: you must participate with God, following His plan for your life.

The prosperity that God has for us is connected to the plans that He has for us. No plan, no prosperity. God's job is to craft a plan for our lives (there's no one better at life-planning than Him). Our job is to discover those plans, embrace them, and align our life with them. We are wrong to assume that just because He has planned it we will fulfill it. This kind of wrong thinking is widespread in the Body of Christ. People everywhere are waiting for God to perform His plans – to do it – while He is waiting for us to discover His plans and walk them out.

The New Testament version of Jeremiah 29:11 is found in one of Paul's writings:

> *But, as it is written, "What no eye has seen, nor ear heard, nor the heart of man imagined, what God has prepared for those who love him."*
>
> *1 Corinthians 2:9*

Again, it's easy to read this verse and rejoice about the great things that God has planned for us. That's great. But we can be happy about this verse every day and still never experience those things. An important part to the equation is found in the next verse:

> *These things God has revealed to us through the Spirit. For the Spirit searches everything, even the depths of God.*
>
> *1 Corinthians 2:10*

It's only when we receive a revelation of His plans that we can walk in the light of those plans. We must not just talk about the fact that He has plans for us, we must discover the details of those plans and walk them out. How is this done? By the Spirit. The Bible reveals the general will of God for our lives, but it's the Spirit who knows all the specifics. He is the Revealer, who takes the things of God (including His plans for your life) and shows them to you (John 16:14). Our job is to receive what He reveals.

How do we receive knowledge from the Holy Spirit? By spending time in the things of God. Spend time meditating and feeding upon His Word so you can clearly discern what's God and what's not (see Hebrews 5:14). The believer must also pray much in other tongues, speaking forth the details of God's plan (1 Corinthians 14:2). Many believers remain ignorant of God's plan throughout their lives because they refuse the great privilege of speaking in other tongues. No one who is ignorant of God's plan will enjoy God's prosperity.

What do believers do who fail to discover God's plan for their life? They fabricate their own plans and ask God to bless them. He graciously complies, but in a much diminished fashion. He cannot bless our plans the way He can bless His plans. When a believer substitutes their plans for God's plans, they are killing their prosperity. God's prosperity is connected to God's plan.

ON THE PATH

Closely related to God's plan is God's *path*. Notice this great verse:

But the path of the righteous is like the light of dawn, which shines brighter and brighter until full day.

Proverbs 4:18

There's prosperity on the path. What if you're not on God's path? You will miss much of your prosperity. If we choose to travel a path other than the one God has designed for us, we lose out on His best (He won't reposition His blessings to meet us). He indeed has amazing things prepared for us, but we only intersect those things as we stay on His path. If we depart, taking detours to suit our own will, we forfeit the blessings that are on His path.

Notice that the path of the righteous grows *brighter and brighter*. That's another way of saying *better and better*. We will experience increase in every area as we progress along the path of God.

Look at this verse in *The Message*:

The ways of right-living people glow with light; the longer they live, the brighter they shine.

God wants our lives to be testimonies of His prosperity, examples of His goodness. Sure, there will be opposition, tests, and trials along the way, but if you are on God's path, things ought to be better today than they were a decade ago. If they're not, it may be because you have veered from His path. A person who is off God's path is away from God's provision. Just spend time with God in the Word and in prayer until you can clearly discern His plan. Then make any necessary adjustments or changes to get back on the path. God will meet you on His path with His blessing.

*For we are His workmanship [His own master work, a work of art], created in Christ Jesus [reborn from above—spiritually transformed, renewed, ready to be used] for good works, which God prepared [for us] beforehand [**taking paths which He set**], so that we would walk in them [living the good life which He prearranged and made ready for us].*
Ephesians 2:10 (AMP)

His plan is too good to miss. The path that He has designed for our life is loaded with good things. The good life is the life that is lived on the path of God.

GOD'S WILL

We've spoken of God's plan and God's path. A third way of illustrating this truth is to say we must remain in God's will. This familiar verse in Romans reveals a key to remaining in the will of God for our lives:

I appeal to you therefore, brothers, by the mercies of God, to present your bodies as a living sacrifice, holy and acceptable to God, which is your spiritual worship. Do not be conformed to this world, but be transformed by the renewal of your mind, that by testing you may discern what is the will of God, what is good and acceptable and perfect.

Romans 12:1-2

Spending time waiting on God (presenting our bodies), and renewing our minds with His Word, is essential if one is to discern God's will for his or her life. Because most Christians do neither of these things regularly, it should come as no surprise that they are not experiencing God's prosperity in its fullest measure. The believer must learn what it means to consecrate (or separate) themselves before the Lord. Only when a person lives a consecrated, dedicated life can they be sure that they are right in the middle of God's will.

INTERSECTING PROVISION

How often do we see Jesus going into a town to minister and, *bam*, He walks right into provision? He was continually intersecting God's provision because He never strayed from God's path. Jesus expected His supply to always be there, and it always was. He knew that as long as He stayed on the path, provision would meet him. He might not have always known where the next meal was coming from, but He knew that it would come. He fed both Himself and His staff for over three years by always being in the right place, at the right time, doing the right thing.

Jesus demonstrated what it was like to trust in God's provision. He taught His followers to do likewise, learning to trust God for themselves.

He charged them to take nothing for their journey except a staff—no bread, no bag, no money in their belts.

Mark 6:8

The religious mind would read this verse and conclude that Jesus was teaching His followers that they didn't need anything temporal or material. No, He wasn't telling them not to have anything, He was showing them how to get something. The staff that they were to take represented the guidance of the Holy Spirit, who leads us into provision. Jesus was teaching them to follow the Spirit on the path of His leading.

When a criminal breaks out of prison, or when a person is missing, there are dogs that can pick up their scent and find them. All that dog needs to do is smell their clothing and he knows exactly who he's looking for. We would say that dog is *tracking* the person's scent.

As believers, we must become accomplished at tracking God's scent, as it were. We must follow Him so closely, that we remain on His path perpetually. That's what He was training His disciples to do; He was teaching them to track God, believing Him to meet every need. What if the Lord did that to you? What if He sent you out with nothing but Him? Could you handle that kind of training? (We would be mistaken to think that the Lord never does that anymore.) How did it turn out for the disciples? Just fine.

*And He said to them, When I sent you off on a mission without a purse and a begging-bag and sandals, you did not lack anything, did you? And they said, **Not one thing**.*

Luke 22:35 (WST)

A PLACE CALLED THERE

When Jesus needed a donkey, it was there. When He needed a place to celebrate the Passover, it was there. He always seemed to know where *there* was.

*And he will show you a large upper room furnished and ready; **there** prepare for us.*

Mark 14:15

*"Go into the village over **there**," he said. "As soon as you enter it, you will see a donkey tied **there**, with its colt beside it. Untie them and bring them to me."* *Matthew 21:2 (NLT)*

If you want the kind of provision that Jesus experienced, you must know where *there* is. *There* is always on the path of God.

> *And the word of the Lord came to him: "Depart from here and turn eastward and hide yourself by the brook Cherith, which is east of the Jordan. You shall drink from the brook, and I have commanded the ravens to feed you **there**."*
>
> *1 Kings 17:2-4*

God is big on this word *there*. Notice that, in this case, *there* meant that the prophet Elijah had to move to a new location. *There* meant leaving what was familiar. *There* was inconvenient. But, *there* is where God showed up.

Here's a great revelation for all of us: we don't get to decide where *there* is, rather, we are to discover where *there* is. If God said go *there*, don't change it and go *here*. *Here* is not *there*. Stay *there*. *There* is best, because *there* is where provision finds us.

People kill their prosperity when they don't look for *there*. They stay in places of fleshly comfort and familiarity and never make the movement or changes that God requires. They ask everyone to pray for them as they struggle through life, not knowing that all the provision they need is on the path. It's all *there*.

> *And after a while the brook dried up, because there was no rain in the land. Then the word of the Lord came to him, "Arise, go to Zarephath, which belongs to Sidon, and dwell **there**. Behold, I have commanded a widow **there** to feed you."*
>
> *1 Kings 17:7-9*

Notice that when the brook dried up, new instructions came.

Now, Zarephath was *there*. If Elijah had said, *I don't feel like moving any more; enough with the journeys; I'm just going to stay here*, he would not have received the supernatural provision that sustained him. The brook was no longer *there*. Zarephath was now *there*. Always make sure that wherever you are, it's *there*.

I've had to go through some mighty uncomfortable situations to stay *there*. I have moved a handful of times, each time uprooting and leaving what was precious to me. However, each time I moved, I knew I was *there*. Often, I would sense the change of direction well in advance. The brook would begin to dry up in my present location. To say, *Let's just stay here* would have been dangerous. Always stay *there* and you'll always enjoy divine supply.

OUT OF PLACE

But as it is, God arranged the members in the body, each one of them, as he chose.

1 Corinthians 12:18

Now you [collectively] are Christ's body and [individually] you are members of it, each part severally and distinct [each with his own place and function].

1 Corinthians 12:27 (AMP)

Here's something else that we must recognize. In seeking God's *plan* and God's *path*, we must also seek God's *place*: our part in the Body of Christ. There is no quicker way to get off God's path than to get out of place in the Body. Think of how unpleasant it would be if one of the organs in your physical body somehow moved out of place. It would certainly affect your life. In the same way, when a person is out of their place in the Body of Christ, it affects their life.

I have met many believers over the years who genuinely loved God and said they wanted His will for their life, yet were out of place in the Body of Christ. Because these truths aren't often taught, believers don't even consider this as a possible cause for the difficulties they are experiencing.

How does one love God but still end up out of place in the Body? The quickest way is to leave the local church to which God had assigned him or her. People have the erroneous idea that as long as they go to *a* church, all is well. That thought is as far from the truth as one can get. Notice 1 Corinthians 12:18 again: God arranges each member in the Body *as He chooses.* Not as we choose, but as He chooses.

There are several different aspects to being in our place in the Body of Christ. First, we must recognize the place to which God has called us. Our place in the Body begins with our place in the local church. If a believer chooses to pull out of church, I guarantee that they are out of their place in the Body, off His path, and away from His provision.

One of the reasons why many leave their church is because of money. They think that pulling away from church will save them money, since they can now keep their tithe. That's nothing but deception. Being out of one's place in the Body is not a prosperity recipe, it's a prosperity killer.

OUR SUPPLY

Another aspect of being in our place includes bringing our supply to our place. Notice that 1 Corinthians 12:27 mentioned *each with his own place and function*. It's not just about being in the right place, we must be functioning – doing the right thing – in that place. We must bring our supply to the Body if we are to prosper.

We used the example of a physical organ being out of place. What would happen if that organ were in place, but stopped performing its function? People, for example, who have had their kidneys cease to function know that it threw their whole body into crisis. We must discern our place in the Body: our location, position, and function. And, we must bring our supply. Failing to do so hinders prosperity.

OTHERS IN THE BODY

Besides being in our place and bringing our supply, we must rightly relate to others in the Body of Christ. It's a Body with *many members*. Every member of Christ's Body has been strategically placed alongside other members. We must recognize and participate in the God-ordained relationships that we have with others in the Body.

The members of Christ's Body depend on each other, much like the organs of the human body depend on each other. We don't always realize how much our supply affects others. Did you know that if the inner ear becomes plugged or infected it can affect a person's balance? Those two areas are seemingly un-related, yet God designed them to be interconnected. So it is in the Body of Christ.

PROSPERITY IS IN THE LOCAL CHURCH

One of the most selfish things a Christian can do is pull away from the local church to which God has assigned him or her. God needs you there, not just for your benefit, but for the benefit of others. When a person gets out of their place in the Body, oth-ers in the Body must do without that person's supply.

Why so much talk about the local church in a book about prosperity? During the years that I pastored, I met many peo-ple who had questions about the problems in their life, many of which were financial. Almost without exception, the root of their problems had to do with their being out of place in the Body. In most cases, they had left the local church in which God had planted them. They would look at me like I was crazy when I suggested that their money problems were the result of their dis-connection from church. Crazy or not, it's the truth. How well would a plant fare if pulled out of the ground in which it had been planted?

There's one final aspect regarding our place in the Body of Christ that we must address. As we relate to others in the Body, we must recognize the place of those over us, willingly submit-ting ourselves.

Obey your leaders and submit to them, for they are keeping watch over your souls, as those who will have to give an account. Let them do this with joy and not with groaning, for that would be of no advantage to you.

Hebrews 13:17

The last phrase of this verse indicates that we will be at a disadvantage if we fail to recognize and rightly respond to those whom God has set over us. If we are at a disadvantage, it will not be well with us. If it's not well with us, we are not prospering.

How many Christians have you met who recognize their lack of submission to leadership as the cause of their financial troubles? I have not met many. Most that I have spoken with would resent hearing that this might be the issue that is holding them back. Rather than submitting to their leaders, many would prefer to blame their leaders for their problems. We must evaluate ourselves in these areas, making changes if needed. We must take our place in His Body, in His will, on His path.

Chapter 16

DOUBT AND UNBELIEF

PROSPERITY KILLER #6: DOUBT AND UNBELIEF

For we walk by faith, not by sight. 2 Corinthians 5:7

For believers to experience God's full prosperity, they must be willing at times to abandon the natural, moving with God into the realm of the unseen and the unknown. Does God really expect us to turn from what we see, hear, and feel in order to go a different way? He sure does. It's called walking by faith, and it's the only way to please Him (Hebrews 11:6).

God is pleased when He is able to bless us, not just according to our desires, but according to His. He longs to bless us *His way,* which is greater than our way (Isaiah 55:9). He stands ready to lead us into His fullness, but we must be willing to go with Him, out into the realm of the unknown.

He will often give a word of instruction, prompt us by the witness of His Spirit, or speak to us through the written Word. Then, as the saying goes, the ball is in our court. We can choose to venture out in faith, or shrink back in fear (Hebrews 10:38). If we draw back, we rob Him from the pleasure that He receives from blessing us.

Let them shout for joy and be glad, who favor my righteous cause; and let them say continually, "Let the Lord be mag-

*nified, **who has pleasure in the prosperity of His servant.**"*

Psalms 35:27 (NKJV)

FAITH QUALIFIES US

As natural parents, we know that it's wrong to indiscriminately give things to a child. They must walk worthy of the blessings we bestow upon them, cooperating with the laws of our home and family. For example, my children have, at times, received some very nice Christmas presents. Those presents were able to be received by them because they were in compliance with our standards and expectations. Had they chosen to rebel and go their own way, the blessings would have been far fewer. It's not that they had to work to earn these gifts, they just had to comply.

Things work the same way where our relationship with God is concerned. No parent has ever wanted their children blessed the way our Father wants us blessed, yet it would be inappropriate for Him do things for us while we walked a course opposite to His. What aligns us with His will, allowing Him to bestow His greatest blessings upon us? Faith. Faith is huge. It's a big deal to God, and finding it in us brings Him great pleasure.

Faith will move out into the unknown with nothing to stand on except God's Word. Jesus required faith from His followers, even when those followers were new to His ministry. (We are wrong to believe that God requires nothing of younger believers. They're often the ones who are flexible and compliant enough to step out and follow God's leading.)

Look at this account from the ministry of Jesus. It speaks of the time when He needed to borrow Simon's boat. Simon is the person we now know as the Apostle Peter.

Getting into one of the boats, which was Simon's, he asked him to put out a little from the land. And he sat down and taught the people from the boat. And when he had finished speaking, he said to Simon, "Put out into the deep and let down your nets for a catch." And Simon answered, "Master, we toiled all night and took nothing! But at your word I will let down the nets." And when they had done this, they enclosed a large number of fish, and their nets were breaking. They signaled to their partners in the other boat to come and help them. And they came and filled both the boats, so that they began to sink.

Luke 5:3-7

GO DEEP

Jesus told Peter to launch out into the deep. What's water like when it's deep? There's nothing underneath you. You feel unstable, surrounded by the unknown, unable to see the bottom to know what's there. Questions abound. The deep isn't fun for the natural senses, but the deep – the unknown – is familiar territory for the person of faith.

This blessing didn't come to Peter and his crew as they were sitting on shore. It came only when they launched out in response to the word of the Lord. First they received the command, then they received the catch. So many people want deep blessings while staying anchored in shallow places. They want to see all the fish before they pull out their nets and launch the boat. When God tells them to step out, they just sit there and ask questions. That's not how faith works. Once God has spoken, you have heard all that you're going to hear. You must act on what He's already said to find out more.

Notice that Peter and his associates sowed seed by allowing Jesus to use their boat. Their seed set them up for their harvest, but their action of sowing wasn't the only action required. They had to put forth effort in order to reap their harvest. They had to sow, and *they* had to reap. God can't sow for us, and He can't reap for us. He can and does, however, multiply our seed sown (2 Corinthians 9:11) and lead us to our harvest.

It takes faith to sow, and it takes faith to reap. Sometimes the faith needed to reap can be greater than the faith needed to sow. Peter and his crew had been fishing all night (the time when fishing is best). They had caught nothing. Everything in the natural – all human reasoning – was against bringing their nets back in the boats and expending the effort to go against the current, out into the deep. If you are going to prosper God's way, however, there will be times when you must make movement while everything in the natural is telling you not to.

Since my wife and I have committed to follow God by faith, I cannot think of a single major purchase that we have made that was justified naturally. By that, I mean God's leadings to make these purchases never seemed to coincide with a time of surplus. Our checkbook and tax return both said we shouldn't have it. If we had consulted other people, they would have told us we couldn't have it. Fortunately, we only listened to God, who had told us it was ours. Always choose faith over sight. If circumstances agree with God, then we need not override them. However, when what God says contradicts what we see, we choose God over the circumstances.

A NEW HOME

The house in which we currently live is an example of launching out into the deep when everything in the natural was screaming *stay put*. This particular home was not even for sale when God dealt with us to purchase it, yet in an unusual way He told us it was ours. What do you do then? Wait for the home to magically transfer into your name? No. Faith makes movement. At God's leading, I contacted the owners. They didn't want to sell at the moment, but were actually preparing to do so soon. The favor of God was upon us and the owner agreed to sell. Within ten days, the home was in our name.

There were a few obstacles along the way. First, the price was higher than I wanted to pay. Even though the home was worth that much, I didn't want to stretch out that far. It was going to take every bit of money I had and then some. To say I couldn't afford it at the time was an understatement. I needed to learn, however, that with God, it's not an issue of price, it's an issue of faith. This home was not in the shallow end, so to speak. It was out in the deep where you have to tread water: constantly moving to stay afloat. My flesh was not comfortable with any of this. My mind was having fits, and I wanted to just get out of the water and sit on the shore.

The owner set up a time for us to meet with him to sign the papers for the purchase. The night before that meeting, laying in bed, I turned to my wife and suggested that we just stay in our current home instead of stepping out into such a big venture. We were, after all, believing for many other things for our ministry and wanted to keep our faith focused on those things.

I went to bed that night thinking I would not move forward with the purchase. However, I woke up the next morning prophesying. (I don't think that has happened with me before or since.) God was encouraging me to step out, showing me by His Spirit how the house would be a blessing for both us and the ministry. That has been the case. He was so faithful to bring me the help my heart and mind needed at the time.

Although God encouraged our faith, He did not force us to step out in faith. He stood out on the water and beckoned us to come (like Jesus did with Peter), but taking that step was entirely our choice. We could have stayed put and been satisfied, but He wouldn't have been pleased. I'd rather please Him than remain comfortable. I want Him to get all the pleasure from my life that He can.

If we desire God's supernatural provision, we must be willing to wade out into the waters of the supernatural. We must be willing to walk by faith, going where we haven't gone before, doing what we haven't done before. God will go before us and lead us into greater prosperity, just like Jesus did when He stood out on the water and bade Peter to come.

Many fail to receive greater levels of prosperity because they simply refuse to step out in faith, abandon the natural, and follow God. They never even pray about the decision, their natural mind dismissing the idea at the outset. This happens all the time with God's people, and it's nothing but plain old doubt and unbelief. Doubt and unbelief kill prosperity.

How it must grieve the Father to watch his children sow sacrificially, but fail to reap a harvest because they lacked the faith necessary to push past natural circumstances. I'm sure there have been things that God has brought to me that I have failed to possess; but I am committed to reaping my harvests, pursuing the opportunities that He brings me.

I'll say it again: if you want God's full prosperity – that which is supernatural and beyond the norm – you must have enough faith to step out into the realm of the unseen and the unknown. God can't get great things to the person whose mind is fixed on the natural, overcome by circumstances.

> *He who observes the wind will not sow, and he who regards the clouds will not reap.*
>
> *Ecclesiastes 11:4*

Wind and clouds represent circumstances in our lives. Like the wind and the clouds, circumstances are always changing. God, who never changes, seems to ignore circumstances when dealing with us regarding prosperity. He will deal with us to sow seed at the most inopportune times. I have yet to have Him ask me, *Joel, is this a good time for you?* No, He deals with me to sow when it's the right time to sow, regardless of convenience. And, He deals with me to reap when it's time to reap, regardless of what else is going on in my life. It may look like there's no way for it to happen, but if it's His will, there's a way.

WINDOWS OF OPPORTUNITY

There are seasons – windows of opportunity – in which to reap certain harvests. If we fail to make movement toward those harvests, the opportunity will be lost. We must reject the thinking that says, *I want my harvest, but I want it my way, according to my timing.* I'm sorry, it's just not going to happen. If you want God's best, you will have to go God's way, following His direction. It's harvest time when He says it's harvest time, not just when circumstances look the most favorable.

*And let us not grow weary of doing good, for in **due season** we will reap, if we do not give up. So then, as we have **opportunity**, let us do good to everyone, and especially to those who are of the household of faith.*

Galatians 6:9-10

The words *due season* and *opportunity* are from the same Greek word: *kairos*, meaning *a God-appointed season.* Although we can certainly give and receive in line with the Word of God in a consistent, regular manner, there are also special God-initiated times of which we must take advantage.

He'll lead us in a special way to give sometimes. That's what the verse is talking about when it says *as we have opportunity.* These opportunities are limited-time offers. Give now, before the window closes. There are also special times where He instructs us to step out and reap: to possess the land, so to speak. That's the *due season* being spoken of. These seasons of giving and receiving are God-appointed, not man-appointed. Our only choice in the matter is whether we will step out and participate, or draw back and go without. I choose to step out. I refuse to step back.

Chapter 17

FEAR OF RUNNING OUT

Faith will look past the natural and make movement, based on no evidence other than a word from God. Doubt and unbelief, on the other hand, will entertain thoughts, questions, and reasonings until all thoughts of moving out in faith are quenched. We must become skillful at bypassing the objections of our mind in order to move forward in faith.

Think about a man named Noah. Before a single animal had arrived, and before the earth had seen a drop of rain, Noah stepped out on nothing but a word from God. To build the ark in today's money would cost well over a million dollars. Noah stopped the work of his previous vocation and, at his own expense, began to work on the ark full time. He spent 120 years building something that was only used for a few months. That's faith.

If anyone today spent the time and money that Noah did for such a short term project, people would call it wasteful. Not God. Noah's project was God's idea. He was perfectly fine with the fact that, once the waters of the flood receded, the ark would sit unused on the side of a mountain forever. We must renew our mind to this kind of thinking. It would shock us to know that, much of the time, God just doesn't care what it costs. He wants the job done, and can handle the cost, whatever it is.

We're the ones that choke over the price of things. If you can't handle paying for a tank of gas, what would you do if the Lord asked you to do something that cost hundreds of thousands, or millions, of dollars? People who are easily upset about how much things cost are not ones God can use for large projects. They don't qualify for great prosperity.

I believe that church buildings will be constructed up until the time that Jesus returns. What if a building costing tens of millions of dollars was completed and used for only a few months before Jesus returned? Who cares? There is such a thing as poor stewardship, but it's never poor stewardship to obey God and do the job right. If God wants us to hold back for some reason, fine, but let that directive come from Him, not from small-minded, penny-pinching believers who choke over spending ten dollars too much.

Smith Wigglesworth was a man of faith, mightily used of God. He would minister in many different places, often traveling by train. On one long trip, another minister on the train recognized him. This minister saw him exiting his drawing room in preparation for arrival at the station. As he greeted Smith, he said, *You know, you could have saved a lot of God's money by sitting up in coach with me.* Smith quickly responded, *I'm not trying to save God's money, I'm trying to save God's servant.* What a great lesson. What liberated thinking.

Our purpose here on Earth is to spread the Gospel, not see how much money we can save the Lord. Nowhere in Scripture do we see the Lord handing out rewards for the ones who saved the most money. When people are that tight with money, they are stingy. They live their lives bound with the fear of running out. People are afraid that if they spend freely, there won't be enough left when they need it. The fear of running out is a by-product of doubt and unbelief. It's a prosperity killer.

What if God deals with you to empty your bank account in order to give a large offering? Prosperity haters would quickly criticize such a thought, saying that the only person who would suggest such a thing is a preacher who is trying to get rich. No, dear friends, God may, at some point during your life, ask you for all that you have on hand. Can you quickly obey, or do the thoughts of upcoming bills prevent you from following through?

Although many would argue that God would never lead a person to give money that is needed for bills, there is no scripture upon which that argument is based. God knows the needs that are ahead of you better than you know them. If He deals with you to sow a certain amount, it's because He wants to be able to supply *all* your needs. He may know that what you presently have is not enough to meet those needs, so He deals with you to sow. As someone has said, if it doesn't meet your need, it may be your seed.

ABOUT TO RUN OUT

I remember a few years back facing a situation where I was quickly running out, with no idea where the supply would come from to meet my needs. I was down to my last several hundred dollars. I don't mean that's all I had in checking. I mean that's all

I had anywhere. The enemy was relentlessly bringing me images of my demise. I decided that if I was to go broke, it would be on my terms and it would be by giving an offering. I found out where a certain minister was preaching, got on a plane, brought that money, and sowed it into the first offering they received. I had to get that seed into good ground as fast as I could.

I had been meditating on the story of the widow who gave her last bit of food to Elisha and was sustained for many days. I needed to be sustained in a similar way, so I just did what she did, giving all that I had. I don't remember everything that happened after that, but I know we didn't run out. We didn't miss a meal. We didn't miss a payment. I had to do something to stop the voices that were trying to move me into fear. Sowing seed is a good way to get the devil to stop talking.

Every believer must overcome the fear of running out. Instead of resisting it, however, many people nurture it. People stockpile things so they'll have plenty for the rest of their lives. They may think that what they're doing will make them prosperous, but what they're doing reveals that they aren't prosperous. Don't get me wrong, I like buying in bulk so I don't have to shop as often, but there's a difference between buying a four-pack of toothpaste and buying an entire palette that's on sale because the expiration date has passed. A rich, full supply and hoarding are not the same thing.

We spoke previously of Depression-era thinking. That kind of thinking shows that a person is bound by the fear of running out. My wife and I have a relative who, for years, had kept a canned-goods collection in the corner of her basement. There were cans of beans, corn, spaghetti, and many other foods that are great to eat during a nuclear disaster. Many of those cans were older than I. Just because you bought the food before they started printing expiration dates doesn't mean that the food is still good.

I MIGHT NEED IT

Why did that relative store all that food? Because she yielded to this thought: *I might need it someday.* Be very careful about that thought. It can kill your prosperity. I don't know about you, but if we get to the place where all that's left to eat is a thirty year-old can of beans, I think I'd rather just die and go on to glory.

Why are people so afraid to throw anything away? Because they think they might need it someday. There are a few situations where that kind of thinking is appropriate. My father-in-law, for example, is a woodworker who keeps a vast inventory of rare woods for future projects. Most people would throw away what he proudly stores in his workshop. His case is understandable, but many others have no such excuse.

When you buy an item at a store, do you get excited when you see what kind of container it comes in? You know, you look past all the pretzels and say, *That jar will really come in handy when those pretzels are gone.* Tell me, what exactly do you plan to put in that jar? And, what about the forty others just like it that you already have? I understand that some people might actually fill those jars up, but with what? Things that should really be thrown away?

When I was remodeling the building for our church in New York, several people helped me with the project. One day, as we were finishing up, I noticed one of our helpers washing out the empty buckets of drywall mud and some empty paint cans. Those empty cans looked so nice and clean that I thought that was a good practice to adopt. From then on, I always washed and kept the empty cans and buckets. By the end of our project, I had dozens, cleaned and ready to go. I never used them, but kept them for years. Why? Because I thought I might need them someday. After all, you can't have too many empty buckets. Actually, you can.

I have met people who are poverty professionals. By *professional*, I mean they have become skillful with small thinking. Some people still have every margarine bowl they have ever purchased. In their minds, they didn't just buy the margarine, they also bought the container. It was like a two-for-one sale. *Look Honey, if you buy this margarine, you get the bowl for free! What a bargain!* That may sound humorous, but this kind of thinking keeps people in poverty for a lifetime. If the world ever runs out of plastic butter tubs, at least we know some people who will be prepared.

Do you save the plastic wrappers and twist ties from your bread? Why? I know, because you might need it someday. The world may get down to their last box of plastic bags, but you'll be prepared. Can you see it now? All the people in your neighborhood who foolishly discarded their bread wrappers will line up at your door to beg a bag from you. You will be the neighborhood hero.

Other people take their running out mentality to even more extreme measures. Some still have every car they have ever owned sitting in their yard, in case they need a part someday. The fact that the parts are rusted and unusable means nothing. Having all those cars in the yard gives them a sense of security: an ounce of relief from the fear of running out.

My dad had sheds behind his house that were full of things that one might someday need (but could never actually use due to their poor condition). As my dad approached his late eighties, I became concerned that when he died, I would have to clean out those sheds. One of the sheds was full of broken lawn mowers, and old cans of paint. Nothing in the shed was usable. The paint cans were metal and were completely rusted through. He kept them, thinking that he might someday need that color paint, but the paint had dried up decades earlier.

Although I understand that natural disasters aren't the work of God, one particular storm was a real blessing to me. When Hurricane Wilma roared through South Florida several years ago, the winds picked up that shed along with its contents. To this day, I don't know what happened to any of it. It may have blown into someone else's yard. That person may have seen all those cans of paint and became excited, thinking, *I'm going to keep this. I might need it someday.*

One of the most ungodly things to hit the screens of so-called Christian television are the survival kits that have been sold in recent years. Renowned Christian leaders were peddling doubt and fear to their studio audience and the rest of the world. They had many different varieties of astronaut food that they encouraged people to store and stockpile. People were told to fill the rooms in their houses with five-gallon jugs of water so they could live two months longer than everyone else when the water supply runs out. Churches were actually teaching their people that their preparedness (AKA fear of running out) would be the witnessing tool that would reap the end-time harvest. Friends, if that's what a Christian is, I'm ashamed to be one.

God has told us in no uncertain terms that He would supply all of our needs (Philippians 4:19). If there's ever a time when we need to pull back, save up, and live on less, God will let us know, and it won't be through a message of fear and doom.

RUNNING OUT OR RUNNING OVER?

It's time to get rid of that fearful, running out mentality. The Bible doesn't say, *My cup runneth out*, it says, *My cup runneth over* (Psalms 23:5). You don't need to keep the shampoo bottle upside down for weeks at a time in hopes that the residue will gather at the opening, providing one more wash. You don't need to add water to the salad dressing bottle to get one more use out of it. God's bigger than that, but He can't bring more to you as long as you are acting like the world is coming to an end.

But they say the economy might collapse. Who's economy? The world's? That's no surprise. The world's economy is on the verge of collapse more often than most of us realize. It's a broken system; a corrupt kingdom. God's economy, however, will never collapse. What if there's a news report on TV that the cost of shampoo is about to triple? Do you use less? Dilute it? Only wash your hair once every other week? Faith will walk away from the television right into the shower, squeeze some shampoo down the drain, and just laugh at the bad report.

> *He is not afraid of bad news; his heart is firm, trusting in the Lord. His heart is steady; he will not be afraid, until he looks in triumph on his adversaries. He has distributed freely; he has given to the poor; his righteousness endures forever; his horn is exalted in honor.*
>
> *Psalms 112:7-9*

I understand that some believers may get furious at this kind of talk. They would argue, *You don't know how hard I have it.* No, you don't know how big God is. The enemy works overtime to deceive in this area, attempting to convince people that the way to have enough is to hold back as tightly as possible. We've already seen how the scriptures powerfully refute that idea (review Proverbs 11:24-25).

LIVING SMALL

When people go through life with little, it's often because they believe small and think small. Anyone can have bigger if they will think bigger. You can have better if you will believe better. I drive very nice vehicles because I have a supply for those vehicles. Could I get by on less? I suppose, but I don't think like that. I'm not trying to get by, I'm trying to get to my destination in the best way possible. If I need something, I don't see how cheap I can get one for, I look to see who makes the best one. That's all I need to know.

Yeah, but the payment is twice as much on that model. That may be true, but what if you only make one payment (paying in full at the time of purchase)? Then does it really matter how much the monthly payments would be? The person who only shops by price will bypass his or her prosperity. Find out what God is leading you to purchase and believe Him for that, regardless of cost. There are many ways He can get it to you if faith is present. There is no way for Him to get it to you if faith is absent. When a person is in faith, God's methods are unlimited. He can get it to you for less, He can cause your income to increase, He can have someone give it to you, etc. Never say, *I can't afford that.* If it's God, He knows how you can afford it and will show you.

Here's something to understand: saving an extra portion of shampoo by going another day between washings is not going to cause more money to come to you. You have a supply for shampoo *when you need it.* If you choose to postpone buying more until you absolutely have to, fine. The supply will be there when you need it. If you use shampoo liberally, as though the container were bottomless, you will need more shampoo sooner. That's also fine. The supply will be there when you need it.

But I only get paid twice a month. Oh, so your job is your supply, not the Lord. That's different. You'd better stretch that shampoo out as long as possible. If a person will learn to look to God as their source instead of their job, God can get what they need to them, regardless of their payday. He really is that big. Too many read Philippians 4:19 and mistakenly think that it says, *But my job will supply half your needs according to the fluctuation of the economy.* You might want to look in your Bible and read that verse again.

Let's be done with small, poverty thinking. Enough with a running-out mentality. It's not a sin to throw things out that you know you'll never use. How about we start in your closet? Have you worn the item in the last year? If you haven't, give it to someone or donate it to a thrift shop. *But what if I need it?* Then buy it again. *But what if I don't have the money to buy it?* Don't allow yourself to think like that. That's doubt and unbelief. The Bible says God will provide, period (Genesis 22:8). Don't allow yourself to think anything else. Thoughts and words of doubt and unbelief will kill your prosperity, keeping you poor. It's not the economy, the circumstances, the bills, or anything else that's bringing you down. You are the only one who can kill your prosperity. Don't do it. Renew your mind to the abundance of God.

Chapter 18

NO MORE SMALL THINKING

Faith knows that the world's worst times can be the Church's best times. Faith will swim upstream to move with God when everyone else is going the opposite direction. Real faith cannot be brought down; it is unconquerable. The challenge for the believer is simply to stay in faith. Doubt and unbelief, faith's counterparts, are subtle, and can creep into one's life unnoticed. We must be vigilant with our faith life, not permitting unbelief or fear. We must stick with the Word of God, saying and believing only what He has said.

Since we have the same spirit of faith according to what has been written, "I believed, and so I spoke," we also believe, and so we also speak.

2 Corinthians 4:13

Develop the habit of monitoring your mouth. Make sure that what you say is motivated by God, not by fear. For example, there's a vast difference between saying, *I don't know where the money is coming from, but I know it's coming*, and anxiously saying, *I just don't know where we're going to get the money*. One of those phrases is filled with faith while the other is embalmed with unbelief and fear. Faith filters what comes out of the mouth. Doubt, on the other hand, just lets it all out.

Doubt manifests itself in small believing, small thinking and small talking. The only remedy for these things is to renew one's mind with the Word of God. If a person will give God the chance, He will help them see like He sees. Think about it: God has never had a need go unmet. He doesn't know what it's like to experience lack. He has never anxiously wrung His hands or furrowed His brow over a debt or obligation. How bold would your faith be if you had His experience and mindset?

One thing I have learned about the Lord is that He will not change who He is to accommodate our small thinking. He doesn't put on an air of poverty just so He can relate to us. Instead, He allows us the privilege of coming up to His level. He requires that we change our thinking to match His. If you spend much time around God, His big thinking will challenge you. He'll talk to you about stuff that costs more than you've ever thought about spending, and when you inform Him how much it costs, He'll just say, *What does that have to do with it?* Neither you nor I will ever succeed in getting God to think small. We will never get Him to agree with the impossibility of our situation.

SPENDING TIME WITH PROSPERITY

If you are open to being stretched and enlarged, God will begin to help you. One way He will do that is by allowing you to be around others who have learned to think big. People of greatness are never small thinkers; it's a privilege to be around them. If you find yourself around such people, walk worthy of the opportunity. I am forever grateful for times, orchestrated by the Lord, when I have been around big thinkers. He allowed me to see how He blesses faithfulness and greatness.

I was invited many years ago to be part of a Christmas production at a large metropolitan church. There were several services, and the musicians were invited up to the executive suite after each service for fellowship and a meal. I knew and respected these pastors, and was excited to see where they conducted their day-to-day business. When I stepped off the elevator into their suite of offices I almost passed out, overwhelmed by the beauty. I'm not sure that I had ever actually been in a room with professionally designed decor, but that was the case with every room in this church.

I walked off by myself, admiring each space, when the Spirit of God spoke to me and said, *This level of prosperity is reserved for my choicest servants.* I realized that He was telling me that, not to exclude me from that level of prosperity, but to encourage me to stay faithful, qualifying for that level myself. All of us can bring the faith and obedience necessary to have God's best. This visit helped me realize just how godly prosperity could be. The rooms weren't just nicely done, God Himself seemed to be present in the decor.

Years later, while attending a series of meetings in another state, the host minister invited all the full-time ministers to his house for lunch. When I saw the house, I was breathless. I had never known a minister who owned a home like that. I was so overwhelmed, that I didn't even walk inside with the others to look around. I just stayed outside, taking it all in. The grounds were as lovely as the home. I was so blessed that God had allowed me to be there.

We ate outside, and after lunch the host minister walked up to the table where my wife and I were seated. He spoke to us privately and said, *I don't bring all these ministers here to flaunt what I have, but to show them how God rewards faithfulness.* Faithfulness. That encouraged me. I wasn't sure that I could ever be as gifted as this minister, but I knew I could be faithful. I began to see that these kinds of blessings weren't just for other people; I could qualify for the same things. God was helping me.

One of my first experiences along these lines occurred while I was on tour with a Christian music group. While enjoying a day off in a certain city, we were invited to the home of one of the church members to relax. This church member was a fashion designer whose sweater designs were worn by the cast of a long running television show in the 1980's. Once the star of this show began wearing these sweaters, they became popular nationwide. As a result, this church member became extraordinarily wealthy.

When we arrived at his home, I began to see things I had never seen before. I stood there in his kitchen staring at an unusual door, wondering what was behind it. The homeowner walked by and said, *That's the elevator. Take it down one flight.* An elevator in a house? That was different. I went down and walked out into an entire floor of high-end sports cars. Not just one or two, but more than a dozen. I had never seen anything like that before. I knew these things existed but assumed that the only people who had them were crooks and drug dealers, not believers and tithers.

For whom does God make all the nice cars anyway? The knowledge required to develop high performance vehicles ultimately comes from God. There's no way for man to invent or discover anything unless God allows it to be revealed. So I ask again, who are the nice cars for? Drug dealers? Who are the nice houses for? Professional athletes who have had nine children with nine different women? No, these things should be enjoyed by God's children. They're here, not for those who lust after them, but for those who qualify for them. One way we qualify is by not choking in unbelief over the nice things on the earth.

I heard one minister tell the story of how he was riding in a car with some other ministers. As they were driving, a beautiful sports car sped past them. One minister in the car commented, *I guess you'd have to do something illegal to be able to afford one of those.* The others agreed. The minister telling this story didn't comment to the others, but thought to himself, *I've had five of those already.* He never would have had even one, however, had he thought like the other ministers in the car. You don't need to gamble, steal, prostitute, or peddle to get nice things, but you must believe big. You must resist small thinking.

Small thinking – a poverty mentality – is rampant in the Church today. Many Christians are on a mission to keep it small, helping the church conserve. If we must use the air conditioner, keep it on 82. If the heat is on, set it to 65. Personally, I'm tired of sweating through my suits in warm weather, or needing to wear an overcoat during the service when it's cool. God is big enough to supply our needs in this area.

Many would say, *How can you think this way when people in other countries don't have air conditioners or cars?* They could have them if they would learn to believe God. Look at these words, spoken by Jesus:

> *For this reason I am telling you, whatever you ask for in prayer, believe (trust and be confident) that it is granted to you, and you will [get it].*
>
> *Mark 11:24 (AMP)*

This verse is true, and will work for anyone, anywhere. Do the things you desire exist? If so, they can be possessed by faith. Thinking that it's wrong to believe God for a nice car because someone else may not have one is poverty thinking. It's like telling your kids to clean their plate because there are starving children in Africa. That makes no sense. No child in Africa has ever been sustained by a child in America eating all of his or her food. That's nothing but poverty thinking, which is the last thing parents need to instill in their children.

People religiously pray, *God, help us be mindful of those less fortunate than us.* He won't do it. He won't help us set our minds on lack and poverty. Why not instead pray, *Lord, help us be mindful of how blessed we are, and help others also receive Your blessing?* There are plenty of resources on our planet for all to be abundantly blessed, if we will learn to think like God thinks.

When a church faces financial needs, the first thing that often comes to mind is, *Let's have a rummage sale.* How about we sow seed and believe God instead of peddling our trash to the neighborhood? Fundraisers may be appropriate at times, but they are not the main way that God funds His works. Let's instead have people tithing, giving, and obeying God, and have some financial miracles.

No more small thinking. Let's think like God thinks so we can have what He has. Let's have more people like Oral Roberts, whose slogan at his university was *Make no small plans here.* Brother Roberts was a big thinker. He built a traveling ministry, then a television ministry, then a university, then a hospital. All by faith.

Let's feed on passages in the Word that show us what God is able to do when His people believe Him fully. Look at the kingdoms of David and Solomon, noting what God did in response to faith and obedience. God is every bit as big today.

Chapter 19

IGNORANCE

PROSPERITY KILLER #7:
IGNORANCE OF THE LAWS OF PROSPERITY

There's a saying in the world: *What you don't know won't hurt you.* The opposite is actually true: what you don't know can kill you. People often say, *Ignorance is bliss.* No, ignorance is ignorant. In the Kingdom of God, *not knowing* is an unenviable position. Knowledge is key. If we want to have more, we must seek to know more.

> *My people are destroyed for lack of knowledge; because you have rejected knowledge.*
>
> Hosea 4:6

God's people aren't destroyed because the knowledge they need is unavailable, rather, they are destroyed because they reject that knowledge once it has been delivered to them. (A person cannot reject something that has never been presented to them. If I reject a delivery, it means that someone tried to get me to accept that delivery.) When God's truth is rejected, a door of entrance is opened to Satan: the destroyer.

God endeavors daily to bring truth to His children, equipping them for success. An alarming number of His children, however, refuse to accept the truth that He brings. Why is this?

Because God's truth often sounds different than the things they have heard all their life. People's religious education keeps them on the outside, looking in, where the blessings of God are concerned. Even born again believers often embrace religion instead of revelation, tradition instead of truth. God's truth, if received, will set a person free from the bonds of religion, allowing them to enjoy the blessings He has richly provided for them.

Prosperity is a subject that has been the victim of mass truth-rejection. Religion simply does not tolerate God's Word in this area. Instead, it replaces the truth with religious teaching and worldly thinking. When religiously educated people hear the pure Word of God, they often spit it right out because it doesn't have the man-made additives they are used to. They refuse to even consider that what they have believed all their life might not be right. Because these people reject knowledge, their lives are subject to destruction.

Destruction, for the believer, doesn't necessarily mean annihilation. Being bound to this world's system instead of functioning in God's Kingdom is a form of destruction. Settling for less than the abundant life He has promised is destruction. Missing out on God's plan is certainly destruction. Anything that subtracts or holds back ultimately destroys. Knowledge from God is the key to avoiding destruction. When people lack knowledge, they are ignorant. Ignorance is a prosperity killer.

THE NATURAL LAWS OF PROSPERITY

Ignorance of spiritual truth will hold a person back from all that God has made available to them. However, there is another side to prosperity – the natural side – that is a necessary area of knowledge for anyone desiring financial success. When people lack knowledge of these natural laws of prosperity (we could call them *financial laws*), their ignorance can be their undoing.

Many years ago, while pastoring a church in New York State, a young couple came to me after our midweek service to ask a question. They were newlyweds, neither one of whom had much skill with finances. They had heard about a Bible-based financial class being offered at another church in our town, and wanted to know if I thought it would be a good idea for them to attend. This class met weekly, for many weeks.

I was familiar with this course and told them that I thought it would be an excellent idea. I also let them know that the material in this course did not represent all of the principles of God regarding prosperity, rather, it just focused on the natural side: saving, investing, financial management, etc. These types of skills are necessary for all people. God can prosper a person supernaturally, but if they don't know how to hold on to the money when it comes, it's all for nothing.

The reason I told this couple that this course only covered one side of the truth is because many people only acknowledge and practice one side. If a person learns faith, sowing and reaping, and confessing, they think that those concepts are all that there is to prosperity. No, there is a natural side as well. (By *natural* I'm not implying that God is uninvolved; He works closely with us in these natural areas.) A person can confess good things all day long, but if they constantly abuse credit cards, for example, they will get in trouble. Casting out *debt devils* is not the answer. Being disciplined with the natural side of prosperity is the answer.

Although the natural side of prosperity is important, it does not dismiss a person from the spiritual side of the truth. People often learn natural financial principles, yet become so rigid with them that they refuse to veer, even for God Himself. While it may be necessary at first for believers to establish hard-and-fast rules for themselves, there may come times when they will have to set aside those rules in order to follow God by faith. Greater prosperity flows when greater laws are in operation. The believer who desires God's full prosperity must learn both the laws of this world's kingdom, and the greater laws of God's kingdom. They must learn both the natural and spiritual sides of prosperity.

CASH VS. FINANCING

Here's an example of what I mean when I speak of people who only operate in one kingdom or the other. Some have purposed to pay cash for everything they buy. That's a commendable commitment, but what if God deals with you to finance a purchase? Are you flexible enough to follow His leading, knowing that He never leads into lack? Having a sound financial plan is important, but following God's Spirit, even if He leads you to sidestep your plan, is how we prosper in God's kingdom.

Many would contend that God would never deal with anyone to finance anything; that God doesn't prosper people by leading them into debt. I understand that thought, and agree that cash is often best, but I also know that God, at times, has clearly led me to finance certain purchases. At other times, He has dealt with me to believe Him for the means to pay cash. Let's be balanced, possessing both natural wisdom and spiritual sensitivity. Some are too undisciplined with their finances for God to ever lead them to step out in faith financially, while others are too rigid in their natural convictions, insensitive to His leadings.

I know of a church that was experiencing a great influx of people and desperately needed a new sanctuary to accommodate them. They had recently hosted a financial expert at the church who taught that no purchase should ever be financed. Consequently, this church decided that they wouldn't build until they had all the cash in the bank ahead of time. This church, while waiting for the cash to come in, lost much of their growth; the momentum that they had enjoyed stalled.

Again, paying cash is great, and avoiding debt commendable, but being led by God's Spirit is paramount. This church could have engaged the people in a building program, keeping their momentum going by financing the construction (if God so directed). There is no one-size-fits-all formula that fits each individual situation.

I was a member of a church that also was experiencing great growth. They felt led to finance the construction of a beautiful multi-million dollar sanctuary. Because this church could accommodate all the people, they sustained their growth, paying off the new building in just a few years. Financing was best in this situation because it was God's plan.

I know of yet another situation where a church was experiencing explosive growth. God dealt with the pastor of this church to build a new 10,000-seat sanctuary, pay cash, and not even receive any special offerings for it. He followed God's lead and all the funds came in. Although God's principles are for all, His specific instruction for one is not His instruction for all. We must learn to be led if we desire His prosperity.

Even from the natural standpoint, there are times when financing can be preferable to a cash purchase. Say, for example, I have $50,000 with which to purchase a new car. I also have an investment with a nice monthly payout of twenty percent. I could pay cash for the car, or finance it through a bank or credit union at an extremely low rate of interest. If I financed the car, I could take that $50,000 and invest it, paying the car payment every month out of the interest I am earning. Once the car is paid off, I would still have my $50,000. If, on the other hand, I paid cash for the car, I would have nothing left to invest. Although we should still seek God for His leading, financing the car makes good financial sense. Those who are ignorant of financial law rarely think of these scenarios.

LEVERAGE

Here's another example of a situation in which financing can be a smart choice. Two people have enough cash saved up to each purchase one modestly priced rental home. Investor A does just that, buying his home outright and receiving a $1,500 rent payment every month. Investor B, however, follows a different strategy. He only puts 25% of his money down on a house and finances the rest. This practice is known as leverage. Leverage means you use someone else's money to move up to something bigger.

Since Investor B only uses 25% of his cash, he has plenty left. For what? Vacation? Nope. He buys three more houses in the same neighborhood, putting 25% down on each. Since Investor B has the added expense of a mortgage, he only collects $700 per house each month instead of Investor A's $1,500. But, since he has four homes, Investor B's total monthly profit is $2,800 instead of $1,500. Almost twice the profit for the same initial investment. That's the power of leverage.

After a few years, Investor B runs into the manager of the apartment complex down the street and learns that the owner is thinking about selling. Investor B makes an offer to purchase that complex, contingent upon the sale of his rental homes. He sells his homes, all of which have appreciated in value. The appreciation from four houses gives him a healthy down payment. Now, instead of four houses, he has 50 apartment units. That's a large enough property to hire a full time manager. Now, Investor B does no work, other than making sure his monthly $15,000 payout is deposited into his account on time.

Both of these investors started out with the same amount of money. Investor A brags to his friends about how, for the last several years, he has been making a healthy profit of $1,500 per month. Investor B doesn't tell anyone (other than the IRS) that he makes $15,000 per month in passive income. Most people wouldn't understand. Tomorrow, Investor A is mowing the lawn at his rental house while Investor B is leaving on a self-financed missions trip. Leverage can be a powerful thing.

It would profit us in the Body of Christ to learn some of these natural laws. Let's stop thinking so much about earning money and instead think more about investing money. What's the difference? A person who earns is working for money. A person who invests has money working for them.

COMPOUND INTEREST

When I was eighteen years old, I received a legal settlement from a corporation that had wrongly accused me of a crime. That settlement was not huge money by today's standards, but it was a decent amount – $40,000 – in the 1980's. My Dad told me it would be best if I didn't just spend all that money, but rather invested it. That sounded like wisdom to me, although I would have been fine just spending it. I was only eighteen and didn't know any better. Thank God for my father's counsel.

My Dad's investment advisor told him about a product that was paying 10% interest, tax-free. Ten percent may not sound like much, but that's a decent rate of return on an investment, even today. My Dad told me there were two ways in which I could collect the interest. I could just leave it in the investment to accrue, or I could receive a check every month in the mail for a few hundred dollars. Which do you think I chose? All I heard was *money in my pocket* or *no money in my pocket*. I'll take the money, thank you very much.

I wish that my Dad had sat me down with a calculator and a sheet of paper and had shown me the result had I let the interest accrue. (Perhaps he tried, but I wasn't interested.) Had I chosen that course instead of choosing to receive the interest every month, I would have doubled my money by the time I was twenty-five. Instead, I had no money by the time I was twenty-five.

When asked by someone what he considered to be the most powerful force in the world, Albert Einstein replied, *Compound interest.* Compound interest simply means that you keep adding the interest that you earn to your total investment, causing your money to multiply faster. As an example, take out your calculator and enter a one hundred thousand dollar investment. Multiply that $100,000 by 1.2, representing twenty percent interest per year: an outstanding rate of return. In one year, you earned an impressive $20,000 on your money, making your total $120,000. Exciting? That's nothing. Press the equals sign another nineteen times, representing nineteen additional years. How does that $100,000 look now, after twenty years? That's the power of compound interest.

The problem with compound interest is that it doesn't just work for you, it can also work against you. When you only make the minimum payment on your credit card, you are likely not even paying all the interest. It compounds, making your balance swell larger and larger. Not understanding the power of compound interest can be a prosperity killer in more ways than one.

There are many other aspects to the natural laws of prosperity that we could talk about, but discussing those would require its own book. I've only provided a few examples to inspire you to take steps to abolish financial ignorance in your life.

Learn how banking and mortgage lending works. Learn at least a little bit about how the stock market works. Learn how taxes work, and try to understand the principles of how to run a business. Know how much interest you are paying on your loans. Don't just ask, *What's the payment going to be?* when looking at an item. That's exactly what the salesman wants you to ask. And please, stop paying top dollar for poor quality.

Christians request prayer for finances more than almost any other thing. If you've ever worked the phone lines at a Christian TV station, you know this to be true. People want someone to agree with them for their breakthrough. They're believing to find a minister with a *debt-busting anointing* and a special word from the Lord. I won't waste my time praying such prayers with people when, in their situation, power from Heaven is not the answer. The word from the Lord that they need is *Balance your checkbook.*

There is a natural side to prosperity, to which all believers must attend. All should understand basic financial and business principles, and have sound financial management skills. Ironically, these basic areas of study are seldom taught in schools. There is also a spiritual side to prosperity, spoken of throughout this book, which is every bit as important as the natural. Those who are ignorant of these natural and spiritual truths will forfeit much of their prosperity.

The Bible provides examples of those who combined natural and spiritual law in order to prosper. One such example is the virtuous woman of Proverbs 31: a woman of excellence, beauty, and skill. Every woman should aspire to Proverbs 31 standards. I love the following scripture, showing how the virtuous woman makes money by engaging in business, and then invests her profits.

> *She goes to inspect a field and buys it; with her earnings she plants a vineyard.*
>
> *Proverbs 31:16 (NLT)*

Chapter 20

WISDOM

The eighth chapter of the book of Proverbs is an exposé on the subject of wisdom. Wisdom is simply the knowledge of what to do in a given situation – the opposite of ignorance – and is a valuable commodity when it comes to financial dealings. Where wisdom is absent, the prosperity killer of ignorance prevails. In Proverbs 8, wisdom is personified, representing Christ, *the wisdom of God* (1 Corinthians 1:24). Listen to the words of wisdom's voice:

I love those who love me, and those who seek me diligently find me. Riches and honor are with me, enduring wealth and righteousness. My fruit is better than gold, even fine gold, and my yield than choice silver. I walk in the way of righteousness, in the paths of justice, granting an inheritance to those who love me, and filling their treasuries.

Proverbs 8:17-21

If, as many believe, money and riches are to be shunned in the Christian's life, this passage is out of place in the Bible. No, the Lord wants us to know with unmistakable clarity that wisdom and wealth are connected. Wisdom from God – the knowledge of what to do – will cause your treasuries (accounts) to be filled. It will bring enduring wealth rather than fleeting wealth. Wisdom is better than gold and silver; we should seek it instead of money. Get wisdom, and silver and gold – money and resources – will follow.

> *How much better to get wisdom than gold! To get understanding is to be chosen rather than silver.*
>
> *Proverbs 16:16*

Simply put, the wise person knows what to do. The one with financial wisdom makes sound decisions. Such a person understands how to properly handle money. They have learned to seek God before making financial decisions. As a result, they almost always succeed. Rarely is there a financial failure.

DON'T BE A FOOL

The opposite of the wise person is the fool. The fool is rash and impulsive with his or her decisions, not worthy to be trusted with great resources.

> *Why should a fool have money in his hand to buy wisdom when he has no sense?*
>
> *Proverbs 17:16*

> *It is not fitting for a fool to live in luxury, much less for a slave to rule over princes.*
>
> *Proverbs 19:10*

People criticize the rich for being rich, often blaming them for the plight of the poor. The Bible, however, paints a very different picture. The reason why the fool fails to live in luxury is not because of the oppression of the rich, but because the fool is a fool.

Fools have little because they lack wisdom, not because they lack money. The answer for the fool who struggles financially is not a handout, but rather instruction in wisdom. If they refuse wisdom (as they often do) they will remain in poverty. Their life as a bottom-dweller is one of their own making. The only hope for a fool is Christ, who is *made to us wisdom* (1 Corinthians 1:30).

We must learn to exercise godly wisdom in all areas of life. Many relentlessly pursue what they think is a path to increase, not realizing the true cost of their pursuits. When a person's pursuits cause them to neglect other important areas of their life, wisdom from God is needed.

We are not to pursue gain at the expense of the things of God, yet many do. The greatest way in which the believer neglects God is by neglecting their local church. When a person has to pull back, or pull out, of their local church in order to spend more time at work, their prosperity will suffer. No matter how hard we work, we will not truly prosper unless we prosper in the things of God.

Another way in which people display a lack of wisdom is by neglecting their families to pursue their career. My spiritual father, Kenneth E. Hagin, would often tell his students that if they won the whole world to Christ but lost their own families, they were a failure. No, we don't put our family before God, but we must put our relationship with our wife and kids before ambition, career, or even ministry.

A third way people fail to exercise wisdom is by overworking, not taking care of their bodies.

Do not toil to acquire wealth; be discerning enough to desist.

Proverbs 23:4

Look at this verse in the *New Living Translation*:

Don't wear yourself out trying to get rich. Be wise enough to know when to quit.

I have known many minsters who have worked themselves to the point of exhaustion in order to fulfill their ministry. It's not that they were trying to get rich, they were just trying to do too much. It does little to help the cause of God when a minister wears himself out and dies young. God simply does not require the believer to run at full speed for long periods of time. Yes, we should give our all for God and bring excellence to His work, but we are not to sacrifice our well being for the sake of a ministry project. We need more of God's wisdom in this area.

SPIRITUAL STRENGTH

Years ago, I was producing a large music project for the ministry I worked for. The songs required complex orchestral-type arrangements, all of which I did myself. I was attending Bible school in the morning, rehearsing singers and instrumentalists in the afternoon, and writing late into the evening. I was also frequently traveling in crusade meetings. As the months rolled by, I began to feel the toll that this project was taking on my physical body. Instead of pacing myself, delegating to others, and resting properly, I continued to run my body hard, pushing past the weariness I was experiencing. It was easy to justify my workaholic mindset; I didn't want to let down the people for whom I was working. Looking back, I can see that this was more likely an issue of pride: a desire to impress everyone with how much I could handle on my own.

As time wore on, my immune system wore out. I completed that project, but in the months that followed, my whole body shut down, leaving me almost bedfast. Doctors told me that most of the remainder of my life would be spent in bed. As a faith person, I refused to believe that report, however, I incorrectly believed that faith meant I must continue to push through and work on. This became a major health issue for me, costing me years of productivity. The only way I was able to recover was to learn to rest and pace myself. I am well and strong today, but it took years for me to learn the balance that would keep me well.

Too many believers *toil* in order to acquire wealth. Toiling implies the absence of God's help. Do you remember Peter's group of fisherman in Luke chapter five? They had *toiled all night but had taken nothing.* Yet, when the word of the Lord came – when God got involved – the fish came. I have learned to avoid taking on projects in the energy of the flesh. If God's not in it, I don't care to do it. That doesn't mean I only do things that are spiritual or ministry related, rather I only do things to which I know God will add His strength. I take time to seek Him and discern His plan. If we will learn to look to Him, having enough wisdom to know when to stop and rest, we will enjoy divine health (physical prosperity). He'll add His strength to both our vocation and our vacation.

Many people, including Christians, spend their health to obtain their wealth, and must then spend their wealth to try to regain their health. Don't spin your wheels in the energy of the flesh, hoping for increase, when you can tap into the increase of God. Look to Him for His wisdom and, instead of wearing out early, you can increase in strength as you go.

BUILDING YOUR HOUSE THROUGH WISDOM

By wisdom a house is built, and by understanding it is established; by knowledge the rooms are filled with all precious and pleasant riches.

Proverbs 24:3-4

This passage is a great encouragement to those who seek to live in God's kingdom rather than staying bound to the world's system. It shows us how to obtain the things which we desire. Receiving knowledge from God and acting appropriately on that knowledge (exercising wisdom) will get your house built and furnished. If wisdom will build your house, it will help you accomplish any other project as well. It will build a business. It will establish a ministry.

Society has taught our kids to believe that the only way to be blessed in the earth is to study hard and become a high wage earner. In other words, go to school and get a good job. That path is indeed appropriate for many, but we are wrong to only emphasize natural education. Not every child has the capacity to become an astrophysicist. (Case in point: I needed my computer's help just to spell that word.) If a child can't understand complex subjects, they are led to believe that they will be relegated to a lower standard of living.

The Word of God emphasizes knowledge, yet not just the kind found in science and math. Unlike our world's system, which focuses only on natural knowledge, God's kingdom operates via spiritual wisdom, knowledge, and understanding. The verse didn't say, *By education a house is built.* That's good news. A person doesn't need advanced college degrees or even a high school diploma to enjoy all the prosperity they could desire. They need only learn to operate the principles of the Kingdom of God. If the Christian will know more, they can have more. If they will understand better, they can have better.

The world's system dictates that the school cafeteria worker could never have what the teacher has, and that the teacher could never have what the principal has. True, there is great income disparity between the three, even though they all work under the same roof. What is a person to do, however, if God calls them to be a cafeteria worker at a school? Are they forced to accept less in life than the principal? The world would say yes, but the Word says no. A person who receives God's wisdom can have all that wisdom brings. You can have your house. Those who gain spiritual understanding can enjoy a blessed lifestyle, regardless of their natural occupation. If a person will increase in the knowledge of God, they can experience increase in every area of life.

Wisdom is the principal thing; therefore get wisdom: and with all thy getting get understanding.

Proverbs 4:7 (KJV)

Chapter 21

SOWING AND REAPING

We have been speaking about the prosperity killer called *ignorance*. Ignorance – not knowing – is no small thing. People are forced to settle for less, enduring years of frustration, all because of what they don't know. My heart, like God's heart, yearns to be able to deliver the truth to people.

While ignorance of financial law can keep a person from thriving in our natural world, ignorance of spiritual law will keep a person locked into the boundaries and limitations of the world, unable to operate in the higher realm of God's kingdom. The greatest prosperity is in the highest realm. Let's do away with ignorance and move on up to God's best. God has prepared great increase for us, but our lives will rise no higher than our knowledge of His laws.

When we speak of natural law, there's no better example than the law of gravity. Gravity keeps everything on our planet from floating away. Although other prominent laws may exist, no one can argue that gravity is among the most important. In the Kingdom of God there are also many laws, some more prominent than others. The scriptures leave no doubt that the premier law in the Kingdom of God is the law of sowing and reaping.

*While the earth remains, **seedtime and harvest**, cold and heat, summer and winter, day and night, shall not cease.*

Genesis 8:22

The lesson is clear: as long as winter follows summer, cold follows heat, and night follows day, harvest will follow seedtime. This is a law at work within the earth. The law of seedtime and harvest, or sowing and reaping, is a spiritual law so powerful that it has become a fixture even in our natural world.

No farmer is surprised when the seed he planted fills his field, yet many weeks passed with the ground offering no visible evidence of harvest. The seed that had been planted multiplied and changed forms, all while underground in an unseen realm. Because farmers know that the law of sowing and reaping works, they plant, confident that in just a short while they will enjoy the fruit of their efforts.

In like manner, the seed of a man can be planted in a woman in hopes of a beautiful baby being born. Once the wife confirms that she is pregnant, life begins to change for the parents-to-be. A baby is being formed in the womb – an unseen realm – while all looks unchanged on the outside. No one is concerned that the parents, who are beginning to shop for baby furniture, are making plans without any visible evidence. We understand how sowing and reaping works. Anyone who has ever been conceived (all of us) is a living example of this law.

If people in our natural world can confidently rely on these laws while lacking outward evidence, why can't believers, equipped for the realm from which these laws originate, have similar confidence? We must become established in the fact that, in the Kingdom of God, whatever we sow, we will reap.

Do not be deceived: God is not mocked, for whatever one sows, that will he also reap. For the one who sows to his own flesh will from the flesh reap corruption, but the one who sows to the Spirit will from the Spirit reap eternal life.

Galatians 6:7-8

This subject affects all areas of our life and is a major component of prosperity. When teaching on this subject, Jesus emphasized the seed's multiplying power. He also emphasized the importance of sowing into good ground. Good seed in good ground yields a maximum harvest.

And other seeds fell into good soil and produced grain, growing up and increasing and yielding thirtyfold and sixtyfold and a hundredfold. And he said, "He who has ears to hear, let him hear."

Mark 4:8-9

PLANTING SEED

Some Bible teachers argue that the concept of *seed faith*, along with phrases like *sow your seed* (in reference to offerings), are misapplications of this spiritual law. They contend that when Jesus taught on sowing and reaping, His emphasis was on sowing the Word of God into our hearts, not sowing a financial seed. It's true, that was the Master's emphasis in this passage, but sowing and reaping is a broad law with application in many different areas. In other places, Jesus taught how this law indeed applies to the area of our finances.

Give, and it will be given to you. Good measure, pressed down, shaken together, running over, will be put into your lap. For with the measure you use it will be measured back to you.

Luke 6:38

The phrase *give, and it will be given to you* is another way of saying *whatever one sows, that will he also reap.* We would be wrong to say that this verse excludes money, yet we would be just as wrong to say that it's only speaking about money. There are many ways in which a person can give. When you give a child your time, you are sowing into that child. When you take your place in the ministry of helps at church, you are sowing seed. And, of course, when you give in a financial and material way, you are sowing.

The smart believer is one that practices this law on purpose. Sow good seed in every area. Sow friendship and you'll have friends. Sow favor and good deals and you will receive the same. Be merciful to people when they miss it and you'll receive mercy. Think of every area in which you want to reap a harvest and then sow good seed in those areas.

WHAT ABOUT REAPING?

Most believers agree with the concept of sowing and practice it in their lives, at least to some degree. Yet, many don't seem to fully embrace the other side of this truth: reaping. We must develop our faith to sow, and we must develop our faith to reap. It's never just sowing, it's always sowing *and* reaping.

What comes after *give?* *It will be given to you.* When you sow a seed, you can speak to it and say, *I'll see you again real soon*. It's coming back to you, transformed, multiplied, blessed.

When we plant a kernel of corn, we don't just reap a kernel of corn, we reap ears of corn, each containing many dozens of kernels. We don't just reap what we sow, we reap a multiplied version of it. It comes back to us good measure, pressed down, shaken together, and running over. Hallelujah! Do we really believe this? Many act as though they aren't expecting anything to come back to them when they sow.

Luke 6:38 reveals an important key to our prosperity and increase. Notice the last part of the verse:

For with the measure you use it will be measured back to you.

It's hard not to get excited about the words *back to you*. When I was a young boy, I would sometimes get one of those wooden paddles with the rubber ball attached. You could smack that ball and be sure of one thing: it was coming right back to you. The harder you smacked it, the quicker it would return. When I was a little older, my parents bought me the grown-up version of that game: a paddleball racquet. I would spend hours hitting that rubber ball against the wall of the court. Every time I would hit it, it would come right back to me because the laws of physics were at work. That's a picture of sowing and reaping. What you do is coming back to you.

Notice the phrase *with the measure you use*. We are the ones who determine the size of our harvest, not God. We set the size of our harvest by the measure we use when we sow. For example, if a neighbor is baking and asks to borrow a teaspoon of vanilla (which we give them), our harvest will be multiplied back to us using the measure of a teaspoon. If, however, we sow with the measure of a dump truck, our harvest would be factored back to us using a dump truck (that's a lot of vanilla). Would you rather have your harvest multiplied by teaspoons or dump trucks? Personally, I like the idea of dump truck harvests.

To put this in terms of dollars, if we sow in five-dollar increments, we would reap our harvest multiplied by five. Sow a five, reap in fives. That's not a bad deal, but it's not the best deal. We can increase the measure by which we sow, thereby increasing the measure by which we reap. Instead of sowing fives, we can sow in hundreds, reaping multiplied hundreds. If we sow in thousands, we reap multiplied thousands. We, not God, are the ones who determine the level of our increase. We set our harvest when we sow.

Notice how vividly the J. B. Phillips translation of Galatians 6:7 reads:

Don't be under any illusion: you cannot make a fool of God! A man's harvest in life will depend entirely on what he sows.

If we really believed this were so – were we simply to take God at His Word (as we ought) – this truth would set us ablaze. We would be looking for ways to sow, believing to give big. Every believer should have a vision to give more and give larger. We should be pressing toward that next level of giving, mindful of the greater level of receiving that is attached. The person who is fully convinced of these truths will become an aggressive giver, even liquidating assets in order to sow.

GIVING AND RECEIVING

*And you Philippians yourselves know that in the beginning of the gospel, when I left Macedonia, no church entered into partnership with me in **giving and receiving**, except you only.*
Philippians 4:15

Jesus, without question, applied the concept of sowing and reaping to finances. Here, we see Paul doing the same. Notice that he viewed their financial gifts as a two-sided transaction: part came to him, and part was coming back to them. It's not just giving, it's giving *and* receiving. Sowing *and* reaping. Ignorance of these two sides of the coin, so to speak, can kill the prosperity that God desires for a person.

Paul goes on to speak further about their harvest: the part of their giving that was coming back to them.

Not that I seek or am eager for [your] gift, but I do seek and am eager for the fruit which increases to your credit [the harvest of blessing that is accumulating to your account].
Philippians 4:17 (AMP)

Was Paul just trying to make his supporters feel good about the gifts they had given, or did he really believe this to be true? Were it anything but the latter, this statement wouldn't be included in Scripture. What an amazing truth. God (among all His other amazing attributes) is the best accountant ever. He knows the detail of every seed you have ever sown: both the amount of the gift and the heart behind it. He multiplied that seed when it went into the ground (when you sowed it), and knows the total in your account right now. Many might think, *I wish I could have some of it right now*. You can. Withdrawing from your heavenly investment account is one of the ways you reap your harvest.

Because Jesus told us to lay up treasure in Heaven rather than on Earth (Matthew 6:19-20), people assume that they can't use any of it until they get to Heaven. That's not a scriptural thought. We can still reap harvests on the earth. We lay up treasure in Heaven when we sow, but we also *lay hold* of what we need here on Earth (see 1 Timothy 6:19). We don't experience the majority of our eternal inheritance here on Earth, rather, we get the first fruits: the down payment (Romans 8:23). That portion is more than enough for anything you or I could ever need.

REAPING

How do we withdraw funds from our heavenly account? ATM? Prepaid credit cards? No, we withdraw by faith. By faith we claim what we need here on Earth, believing that we receive it when we claim it (Mark 11:23-24). That's how we lay hold of our harvest.

During an extended time of prayer and seeking God, the Lord gave Rev. Kenneth E. Hagin this revelation regarding prosperity. He told him: *The money you need is on the earth. I don't have any American dollars in Heaven. Just claim what you need from this world's system.* The Lord was essentially telling Brother Hagin,

Stop asking me to do something about your harvest. You do something about it.

Many have sowed great seed but have seen little in the way of harvest. That's because they mistakenly believe that reaping is God's responsibility: that He just takes care of it. That was Brother Hagin's error. He kept praying for God to bring him the money he needed, while God was waiting for him to lay hold of his supply by faith. Although God is involved, reaping is our responsibility, not His. When needs present themselves, we must take the initiative to reap our harvest.

After His teaching on sowing and reaping in Mark 4, Jesus spoke these words, bringing even greater clarity to the subject:

And he said, "The kingdom of God is as if a man should scatter seed on the ground. He sleeps and rises night and day, and the seed sprouts and grows; he knows not how. The earth produces by itself, first the blade, then the ear, then the full grain in the ear. But when the grain is ripe, at once he puts in the sickle, because the harvest has come."

Mark 4:26-29

Notice that parts of the harvest are the responsibility of the farmer, while other parts are more or less beyond his control. Who plants the seed? The farmer. Who causes the seed to spring up and grow? That part happens automatically *(The earth produces by itself)*. But then who reaps the harvest? That's also the farmer's job. He puts the sickle in.

This is an important concept to understand. Most expect God to bring their harvest to them, but that's not how it happens in the natural. Have you ever heard of a harvest of crops jumping out of the field into the barn all by itself? No, the farmer must put in his sickle and reap if those crops are going to come in. Likewise, we bear the responsibility of reaping if we are to enjoy our financial harvests.

Many refuse to entertain these truths because they have been taught never to presume upon the Lord. They believe that if God wants them to have something, it will just show up. That belief is inconsistent with the laws of sowing and reaping as taught in Scripture. You can have a garden of ripe vegetables, but sitting at the dinner table praying for something to eat won't get the veggies on your table. You must go out to the garden, pick the vegetables, wash them, cook them, and serve them if you want to enjoy your harvest. Both naturally and spiritually, reaping takes effort.

We reap with our faith, claiming what we need from this world's system. Our mouth is the *sickle*, calling our harvest in. We sow, God gives the increase, and we reap. Yes, God will lead us to our harvest and let us know when it's time to put the sickle in, but we are the ones who must release our faith. God cannot release faith for us; He cannot reap our harvests.

PATIENCE

Cast your bread upon the waters, for you will find it after ***many days***. *Ecclesiastes 11:1*

*They do not say in their hearts, Let us fear the Lord our God, who gives the rain in its season, the autumn rain and the spring rain, and keeps for us **the weeks appointed for the harvest.***

Jeremiah 5:24

*Be patient, therefore, brothers, until the coming of the Lord. See how the farmer waits for the precious fruit of the earth, **being patient** about it, until it receives the early and the late rains.*

James 5:7

The uncomfortable thing about sowing and reaping is the time that must pass between the two. As Ecclesiastes says, there are *many days* between seedtime and harvest. Our flesh doesn't like having to wait; it wants everything now. There is a way, however, to regularly experience harvest: always sow seed. If a person is sowing something every day, chances are they will be reaping something every day. You can have a continual harvest if you will continually sow.

No one in God's family should be ignorant of these laws of sowing and reaping. God needs all of us cooperating with these laws: sowing good seed and reaping great harvests. Let's be generous sowers, so we can reap large, bountiful harvests.

He who supplies seed to the sower and bread for food will supply and multiply your seed for sowing and increase the harvest of your righteousness.

2 Corinthians 9:10

Chapter 22

LAZINESS

PROSPERITY KILLER #8: LAZINESS

The mere passage of time does not ensure prosperity. It's easy for a person to see themselves prosperous ten or twenty years from now, however, we must not practice deferred faith: putting off until tomorrow what should be believed and possessed today. If a person doesn't see themselves prosperous today, they won't be prosperous in ten or twenty years.

Faith takes effort. In order to keep the proper image formed on the inside of a person, there must be constant input from the Word of God. If a person will see themselves as God says they are – rich in every way (2 Corinthians 9:11) – their life will conform to that image. We become what we behold. Each person's life today is a reflection of the picture they have carried around inside them in years past.

Most Christians are broke instead of blessed, but the reasons why are far less complicated than people care to believe. It's not that the devil has chosen to work overtime on them. It's not because a spouse left, the economy shifted, or the local plant closed down. These things might affect a person temporarily, but none can kill their prosperity. People in the Body of Christ who have been enlightened to the truth often suffer financially simply because they are too lazy to build the Word of God into their spirits. Laziness is a prosperity killer.

Of course, there are many Christians who have not been enlightened to the truth. They are in churches that teach against prosperity, listening to leaders who formulate religious sounding excuses for the difficulties of life. These ministers convince people to accept as the will of God every circumstance that arises. Their theology is reflected in statements such as *When God closes one door, He opens another.* Such teachings are commonly accepted, but are not supported by Scripture. They are an excuse to do nothing, to remain spiritually lazy. We must choose to believe God's written Word rather than church creed.

God leads us through life in accordance with His plan, but His plans often take us down roads that look like dead ends. He will lead us into impossibility for the purpose of proving our faith, glorifying Himself as He works the miraculous. We don't sit idly by, waiting for God to open doors, rather, we boldly press into the things of God, steamrolling the opposition of the enemy. We will never experience the prosperity and victory that we should if we are lazy. We must be proactive rather than passive.

The Bible says much about the prosperity killer we call *laziness.* The scriptures refer to the ill effects of natural laziness, but spiritual laziness is equally deadly. Additionally, there are other areas in Scripture that are closely related to laziness. We'll look at a few of them.

DISCIPLINE

A little sleep, a little slumber, a little folding of the hands to rest, and poverty will come upon you like a robber, and want like an armed man.

Proverbs 6:10-11

This verse, of course, is not teaching that it's wrong to rest, for we know rest to be an essential part of life and faith. I believe that there are times when the most spiritual thing a person can do is get some sleep. Overworking is the cause of much sickness in a person's life. Of course, laziness is the ditch on the other side of the road. Both extremes must be avoided.

When an adult man or woman regularly goes out until all hours of the night, watches movies for hours on end, sleeps past noon and plays video games the rest of the day, they have a discipline problem. God's plan for our lives includes rest, but He does require us to be productive. We don't have time to waste. The lives of many are fraught with laziness.

We must strictly discipline ourselves, developing good habits in both our natural and spiritual life. If a life of discipline hasn't been your habit, ask God to allow you to spend time around someone who is disciplined: someone from whom you can learn a more regimented lifestyle. Too many believers fail to discipline their spirit, body, or mind with enough regularity to realize a difference. It's not what a person does once that brings change, it's what they do consistently.

Notice the high degree of importance that the Apostle Paul placed upon discipline in his personal life.

I discipline my body like an athlete, training it to do what it should. Otherwise, I fear that after preaching to others I my-self might be disqualified.

1 Corinthians 9:27 (NLT)

DILIGENCE

A slack hand causes poverty, but the hand of the diligent makes rich. He who gathers in summer is a prudent son, but he who sleeps in harvest is a son who brings shame.

Proverbs 10:4-5

Diligence is the opposite of laziness. The diligent person is one who is on the case, at the helm, and in-the-know. The diligent person puts forth effort without being forced. He is his own disciplinarian. He manages his time and maintains healthy balances in life. He makes time for his family and allows time to exercise his body. He is the opposite of the person who walks around with their head in the sand. He can tell you what's owed and what's come in. The diligent person is a prosperous individual.

Whoever is slothful will not roast his game, but the diligent man will get precious wealth.

Proverbs 12:27

This is interesting. The slothful (lazy) man doesn't roast his game. That means he killed some game, but somehow was not organized or motivated enough to get it home, cleaned, and grilled. We've all met people who love to start projects but can't seem to finish them. They enjoy the idea of success, but not the work. Purpose never to be such a person. They will not prosper.

My father-in-law decided one spring to create an enormous vegetable garden in his back yard. Tomatoes, zucchini, squash, peas, beans, corn, etc. You name it, he could grow it. He built elaborate fences to keep the wild animals out and tended diligently to that garden for several years. However, each year, just before harvest time, he would go away on vacation, leaving all the vegetables. My wife and I would have to go over to his house and pick everything we could before it rotted in the ground. When I read the scripture about not roasting your game, I always think of the un-reaped garden at my Father-in-law's house.

The soul of the sluggard craves and gets nothing, while the soul of the diligent is richly supplied.

Proverbs 13:4

The lazy person desires prosperity but doesn't want to exert prosperity's effort. The lazy person (the sluggard) craves, but gets nothing. He desires but does not receive. He thinks that just having the right desires will get the job done; that if he wants something badly enough it will somehow just show up. It will not. The diligent person, on the other hand, has a rich, full supply. We must learn that desire is not the same as discipline and diligence. We cannot substitute desire for natural and spiritual effort.

Notice another verse that speaks to this same truth:

The desire of the sluggard kills him, for his hands refuse to labor. All day long he craves and craves, but the righteous gives and does not hold back.

Proverbs 21:25-26

It's important to have vision and desires, but we must not stop there. Wanting something is not the same as exercising faith for something. The righteous person does the work of faith by giving from a generous heart, while the sluggard sits idly by, wishing and dreaming. The righteous and the sluggard no doubt share many of the same desires, but the righteous receives while the sluggard does not.

IT TAKES TIME

Diligence implies consistency over the long term. The Bible speaks clearly of God's increase as something that occurs over time, rather than something that happens instantly. Yes, God does do some things instantly and miraculously, but those things will only be enjoyed by the believer who has been diligent to put forth faith's effort, not by those who just sit around wishing for change. Lazy Christians do not want to hear about things happening slowly. They want it now, they want it easy, and they want it without effort. What does the Bible say along these lines?

Wealth from get-rich-quick schemes quickly disappears; wealth from hard work grows over time.

Proverbs 13:11 (NLT)

The plans of the diligent lead surely to abundance, but everyone who is hasty comes only to poverty.

Proverbs 21:5

God's increase is slow and steady rather than quick and easy. Although it might not come quickly, it will happen *surely*, meaning that diligence over the long term guarantees success. I'll take that guarantee. The Bible says when we exercise diligence we will *surely have abundance*. Glory! We are wise to remember these verses when we hear ministers making outlandish promises in exchange for lavish gifts. Such practices are the Christian version of get-rich-quick schemes and are not promoted by Scripture.

MIRACLE BREAKTHROUGH OFFERINGS

Would God ever tell a minister to promise people a certain kind of return on their money? It's possible, but unusual. It's certainly not the way God normally works.

Having been in a lot of services, and having spent over a decade on Christian television, I have heard many ministers promise a miracle to people in exchange for an offering. On very few of those occasions was it evident that God was in it. Why, then, would ministers do these things? Are they trying to hurt or rob the people? Not usually. Ministers do these things because they work. When people haven't been taught the Word, ministers turn to gimmicks to bring the money in. A large part of the Charismatic Christian community are gullible people who love to get excited about something far out and spectacular. Many of them only give when the promise of a miracle breakthrough is attached.

Understand this: there is no *miracle breakthrough anointing* on any minister's life that can overcome the prosperity killers in your life. Prosperity killers are more powerful than any prophetic word from the Lord. If a person is yielding to qualities such as laziness, stinginess, ignorance, or covetousness, no blessing from Heaven can prevail. The prosperity killers must be removed – neutralized – for the power of God to flow and the blessing to result.

Don't misunderstand me. God can be mightily involved in an offering. He can specially anoint a person to receive a particular offering. God's Spirit has come upon me at times for this very task. Never once in all these years, however, has God dealt with me to extend any kind of extreme promise to the people. The reason He hasn't is that not everyone in the room qualifies for miracle provision. Let's not feel the pressure to bring something unusual, different, or *special* to the people. Let's just teach God's Word, proclaim His promises, and allow the people to participate if they want to. If they do, they'll be blessed.

Brother Hagin was such a great example to me in this area. He would receive offerings, often making this statement: *You can give or choose not to give. Nothing extraordinarily wonderful will happen to you if you do, and nothing terribly bad will happen to you if you don't. If you give, you're not going to become a millionaire overnight, but God will honor His Word and you'll be blessed. And, if you don't give, your pet dog or pet cat is not going to die.* He believed in giving people the Word and letting them make the choice to believe and act upon that Word. I'm glad to have had such an example to follow.

DISTRACTIONS

Whoever works his land will have plenty of bread, but he who follows worthless pursuits lacks sense.

Proverbs 12:11

For the believer, a worthless pursuit is any activity or project outside the plan of God. Many are quick to follow that which seems to be new and fresh, not realizing that, for them, it's worthless. These worthless pursuits are distractions to the believer, and have sidetracked many.

When my son was about six years old, we enrolled him in a swimming class that met at the local high school. His class was a half-hour long, and he usually enjoyed participating with the other kids his age. The problems began after the class was over.

My son, by this age, knew how to dress himself just fine. I would help him change into his swimsuit before the class so he wouldn't be late for his session. After he came out of the pool, I would tell him to go *quickly* change in the locker room and bring me his wet suit and towel. I would watch as child after child emerged from the locker room, yet my son was nowhere to be found. Finally, as the next class was dismissing, I gave up and went back to see what was taking him so long. I expected to find him struggling with his last shoe or sock, but there he stood, naked, playing with the lockers or reading every sign in the room. At this stage in life, staying focused on the task at hand was beyond his capacity.

Many believers have similar issues when it comes to taking

care of business in their own lives. They let the smallest distraction pull them from their task. Three hours later, they ask themselves, *Now, what was I doing?* If the believer isn't careful, distractions can turn to destruction. A person's whole life can pass them by, until it's too late for them to fulfill God's plan. We must develop a focus that refuses to be pulled off-task. Only then will we fulfill the plan of God and enjoy full prosperity.

DISORGANIZATION

Know well the condition of your flocks, and give attention to your herds, for riches do not last forever; and does a crown endure to all generations?

Proverbs 27:23-24

It's important that we know what's going on in our life and finances. Many do not. To them, every bill is a surprise, tax time an annual crisis. If we desire prosperity, we must do better. We must *know well the condition of our flocks.* Those who don't will quickly discover that having something and keeping something are two very different things.

We have been taught to focus on the God-realm rather than the natural realm, but the natural does require our attention at times. Those who have forsaken the natural think that they're being spiritual when they're really just being lazy. For example, we know that we should cast our cares upon the Lord, avoiding worry. That practice, however, can be taken too far. What some people call *casting their cares* is really denial, irresponsibility, and plain old laziness. People use faith as an excuse to avoid facing reality. We need not be obsessed with the natural, but nor are we to ignore it. We must stay on top of our finances, *giving attention to our herds.*

I'd like to share an example of laziness and disorganization from my own life. Enjoy it, for it cost me a lot of money.

I don't have too much experience with the stock market, but I do own some stock that I bought several years ago. I knew that this stock had never really varied much in value, so I left it alone, believing that it would eventually grow. After many years, I sensed a leading from the Lord to sell this stock. I took a quick look on my computer and saw that I would make a few thousand dollars if I sold.

Selling this stock was an involved process, as I had to pay to convert my certificates into a tradable form. I finally got this done and again checked the price. No change. Since it wasn't doing much I let it sit for several more months. Eventually, I decided that I should obey the leading that I had received months earlier. I took a closer look on the computer and experienced quite a shock. Had I acted promptly on the Lord's leading, I would have indeed made money. Now, I discovered that my stock had lost all its value. It was practically worthless.

Was this God's fault? No. He led me to sell when there would have been a profit. I just wasn't organized enough to follow through in time. It took me months to take care of something that should have taken just a week or two. I wasn't paying attention to my herds, and wasn't paying enough attention to the leading of the Lord. Instead of making a few thousand dollars, I lost several thousand. All because of disorganization.

Not knowing what is going on financially with a business or ministry can kill it. Some are so disorganized that they pay every bill late. I know of an accountant who kept books for several ministries. This person told of one client who, in just one year, had paid over ten thousand dollars in credit card late fees. That kind of mismanagement will kill your prosperity. Do we really expect God to deal with people to sow into a ministry that is too disorganized to keep track of their obligations?

A lot of people have too much going on. They either need to cut back or hire some help. There are bookkeepers that can be hired for just a few hours a month to reconcile accounts. Don't be like I was. For years, I never opened my bank statements when they came in the mail; I just threw them in the trash. Is it any coincidence that during those years I never had much? Why would God trust me with more when I was lax with what I already had? I'm thankful that the Lord has taught me these principles, and that I have learned to take these things seriously.

I pastored a church in New York State for eleven years. My wife and I pioneered that church, meaning that we started from scratch and watched God add to us. One of the first things that I did when starting that church was to meet with an accountant, who helped me set up a system of bookkeeping.

I didn't have anyone else to help me with the books, so I learned to keep them myself. In all the years that I pastored, I always knew, to the penny, what was in our accounts. I had to become better organized and more disciplined in order to prosper. I couldn't let disorganization kill my prosperity.

People who are disorganized in life are often spiritually disorganized as well. They have decisions and issues stacked up on the inside of them that they have never yet prayed about or dealt with. They are scattered and unfocused. Until they deal with these things one at a time, they will continue walking around in a cloud of confusion. If a person will get things in order spiritually, they will have a much easier time becoming organized in the other areas of their life.

A key to experiencing organization throughout your day is to put the things of God first. When you wake up in the morning, turn your heart toward God, spending some time fellowshipping with Him in prayer. Spend time in the Word early in the day. It will be shocking to see how much more can be accomplished when the things of God are first.

TAKE IT

From the days of John the Baptist until now the kingdom of heaven has suffered violence, and the violent take it by force.
Matthew 11:12

Here, Jesus shares that there is a survival-of-the-fittest element to our Christian walk. Much of God's provision in our life comes as we lay hold upon His promises and, by faith, take what's been provided for us. Notice, I used the word *take*. When the Bible speaks of receiving from God, the literal meaning of the word *receive* is *to take*. Here's an example:

*Therefore I tell you, whatever you ask in prayer, **believe that you have received it**, and it will be yours.*

Mark 11:24

This verse would be more accurately translated if it said *believe that you take it*. Are we really to take from God? Yes. We are to take that which He has promised and offered us, laying hold of it with our faith. Many would reject such a thought, finding the idea offensive and presumptuous. Most Christians believe that we should wait for God to hand-deliver our blessings to us, rather than taking them ourselves. That's wrong thinking.

When God issues a promise to us in His Word, and we act as though He didn't really mean it, that's offensive to Him. How would a parent feel if they prepared a wonderful buffet-style meal for their family, but all the children just stood there looking at the food, wondering if it was really okay to make themselves a plate? Something would be seriously wrong with that family.

How does God feel when He makes provision for us through His Word, tells us to *come-and-get-it*, and then watches as we sit there, afraid to help ourselves? That's a sad sight indeed. Every parent (God included) would gladly prepare a plate and deliver it to their little ones who aren't yet capable of helping themselves, but the older, more mature children are expected to come and take. If a person insists on waiting for God to come deliver their blessings to them, we know that they are a spiritual baby.

In the Kingdom of God, if you want what belongs to you, you must boldly come, and aggressively take. The things of God do not just fall into our lap. We take what belongs to us *by force*.

What kind of force is this speaking of? The force of faith. That's what we're violent, or aggressive, with. We come with the promises of God in our mouth and claim our needs met. The sound of faith-filled words proceeding from our mouths is a force that can shake Hell and release blessings from Heaven.

A series of famous science-fiction movies coined the phrase *Use the force*. In those films, *the force* was the power that got things accomplished. That force didn't work automatically, but only as the warriors trained themselves to cooperate with it. The spiritually lazy Christian doesn't want to bother with training or learning, so they find a church that tells them that there is no force, that it's wrong to take. These kind of churches promote the lie that my first church taught: *if God wants you to have it, you'll have it*. No you won't. You'll only have it if you take it.

Israel was spiritually lazy. They wanted God to do everything for them. God didn't ask much from them – He just needed their cooperation – but they wouldn't hear of it. They preferred to waste their energy, bawling and complaining about how big the giants in the land were. Even when they finally arrived in the promised land they procrastinated, only possessing what God gave them when firmly rebuked.

> *So Joshua said to the people of Israel, "How long will you put off going in to take possession of the land, which the Lord, the God of your fathers, has given you?*
>
> *Joshua 18:3*

Religion teaches people to sit back, wait, and see. It teaches us never to presume upon God, never to be aggressive. We must reject that type of thinking and instead act like my dogs act when some food is spilled on the floor. Once that food hits the floor, they know it's in their domain, and rush to be the first one to lick it up. God has placed His blessing in our domain. We must not be passive nor complacent, but must rather fight the good fight of faith, seizing what God has said is ours. Use the force. Find out what belongs to you, and take it.

Chapter 23

CARNALITY

I stated earlier that one doesn't need to succumb to all the prosperity killers in order to disqualify from God's best. They need only yield to one. Here's the one killer that often affects people that are otherwise well-taught and on-the-case. A person can be diligent, educated, even generous and faithful, but still be carnal. Carnality is a prosperity killer.

The word carnal, used in the *King James Version* and other early English translations, means *flesh-ruled*. When a person is ruled by their flesh instead of by their spirit, we would say they are carnal. You don't have to travel very far to find a carnal Christian. In fact, you might not even need to leave your house to find one! Because all of us have flesh, all of us must deal with the desires of the flesh; all must deal with carnality. The flesh wants to be in control and doesn't easily relinquish that control. The only recourse? Crucify it.

Most in the Body of Christ are carnal rather than spiritual. The spiritual person has a huge advantage over the carnal person, especially when it comes to hearing from God. The spiritual person is a Spirit-led individual. The carnal person is not.

The Lord is my shepherd; I shall not want. He makes me lie down in green pastures. He leads me beside still waters. He restores my soul. He leads me in paths of righteousness for his name's sake.

Psalm 23:1-3

People, saved and unsaved, love Psalm 23, but few understand its message. Notice the phrase, *I shall not want.* That means we shall not experience lack or go without. It means we will prosper, enjoying constant provision. The promise of a life without lack is wonderful, however, it is not experienced without understanding the first part of this verse: *The Lord is my shepherd.*

Shepherds have one main job where sheep are concerned: they lead them. They keep watch over them, guiding them toward right places and right activities. This passage speaks of *green pastures* and *still waters*, depicting lush provision and undisturbed peace. Little white fluffy sheep aren't the only ones who need a shepherd. Christians also need a shepherd: the Lord. How is He a shepherd to us? He leads us through life. He leads us away from lack, into provision. He instructs us, teaches us, and counsels us, so that we go the right way, do the right thing, and make right decisions.

I will instruct you and teach you in the way you should go; I will counsel you with my eye upon you.

Psalms 32:8

Hearing from God – being led by His Spirit – is essential to prosperity. If I were asked to single out one of the many areas that we have spoken of as the most important, it would without a doubt be this area. If a person can hear from God, they can always succeed. If they can't hear from God, they're in trouble. The carnal person is severely disadvantaged because they are not spiritually sensitive enough to hear from God. They make decisions on their own, based on worldly counsel, natural circumstances, and mental reasoning. That's no way to live if you want the prosperity of God.

I have made it my life's pursuit to be led by the Spirit. I'm convinced that it's possible for a person to never miss it if they will learn to be led. There have certainly been times when I have missed it, making a wrong decision, but even those times were invaluable from an instructional standpoint. To be able to look back and know exactly why you missed it (recognizing that you went against God's leading) is priceless, even when that knowledge came at a cost.

Remember the revelation that Rev. Kenneth E. Hagin received from Jesus along these lines. The Lord told him, *If you'll learn to follow My Spirit, I'll make you rich.* I watched Brother Hagin follow the Spirit's leadings for many years, and saw how God brought increase into his life. He was very well provided for, able to give tens of thousands of dollars at a time to the work of God.

I realized that if I learned to follow the Spirit, I too could be rich. (I understand that the Lord has already made us rich, however, I am speaking of experiencing the manifestation of it in our lives.) I have endeavored for years to be led in my financial decisions and, although there are still more levels of increase ahead, I can truly say that the Lord has made me rich. By that, I mean He has brought His blessings into my life in a way that far exceeds anything I could have planned. I am not covetous, I am rich – fully supplied – and it's wonderful.

Rich is a relative term, with different meanings for different people. Everyone can have a full supply (which is what the word rich means), yet fullness of supply can be experienced at many different levels. What one person might consider a rich supply might look like poverty to another person. There are different levels at which one can be rich. We must not only look at our own personal level of wealth as an example of what it means to be rich, but should celebrate God's full supply at every level.

For example, I live in a comfortable home, but not a ten million dollar home. That's a different level of house, requiring a different level of resources than I currently possess. Am I believing to move up to a ten million dollar house? No. My current home keeps my faith plenty busy, and I have no desire for greater at this time. However, God may someday lead me to a home of that caliber or price. His leading instantly changes my desires. If He's in it, I want it. If He's not in it, I don't want it.

LED IN EVERY DECISION

I remember when I first became serious about following the Spirit's leadings. The Lord had dealt with me by His Spirit to pastor a church, yet I didn't know to which city, state, or country He was calling us. My wife and I took extra time to pray, endeavoring to discover His plan. Because this was an ongoing season of prayer and preparation, I learned to constantly stay sensitive to my spirit; I didn't want to be carnal and miss out on His leading. When we finally sensed that He was leading us to pastor in Buffalo, New York, we knew that we were hearing Him accurately.

After we moved to plant our church, I was faced with more decisions, all of which were critical. One wrong decision could cost us dearly. I again pressed into God on a more continual basis so as to hear Him most distinctly. It eventually dawned on me that big decisions would be an ongoing part of my life. (When leading a church, decisions often affect many other people.) I decided to live close to God all the time, so as to never be far from His leadings.

I have learned to look to God for His help in every decision; not just large, spiritual decisions, but even smaller, natural decisions. What do I order off the menu? Yes, I'm serious. I don't need to travail in prayer about it, but if I'm at a new restaurant and don't know what's best, why not look to the One who does know? I just check down in my spirit and see what I have the most peace about.

If I'm out at a shopping plaza and see something I might want, or that I might want to buy my wife, I check my spirit. Just because I might have the money doesn't mean buying the item is the right thing to do. I might need that money tomorrow for something more important that I don't yet know about. God, however, knows all, and will lead us in every area in which we choose to look to Him.

How do I know when to buy a new car? God leads me. How do I know which car to buy? He instructs me and teaches me in the way that I should go (Psalms 32:8). How do I know which plane tickets to buy, or which plane to buy? I'm led. God knows if there will be a weather issue (or other issue) that would hinder my trip, and will lead me to the green pastures of prosperity and safe travel.

If we will be led in small, everyday decisions, we will not be overwhelmed when bigger issues arise. We will be able to hear from God with clarity and move forward with confidence.

How, practically speaking, does one hear from God and experience His leadings? The main way that God leads us is through the witness of His Spirit (Romans 8:16). What is that witness like? It is a manifestation of the peace of God in a person's spirit. When His tangible peace comes alongside your decision, you are being led. You are hearing from God.

*For you shall go out in joy and be **led forth in peace**; the mountains and the hills before you shall break forth into singing, and all the trees of the field shall clap their hands.*

Isaiah 55:12

We must not minimize this precious commodity of the peace of God. It's how God guides us through major decisions. When we become familiar with His presence, we will experience His peace. We can tune into His peace so distinctly that it becomes a constant voice in our lives.

I continue today to make decisions by looking to His leading, following His peace. He has never led me wrong and He will never lead you wrong. The answer for every question in life is,

Be led. We put the written Word first, understanding that God's Spirit will never lead us contrary to the teachings of Scripture, however, in all the details of life, we can expect to be led by God's Spirit.

Being led is how we reap our financial harvests. The Spirit of God will lead us to our harvest, letting us know when it's the *due season* to step out and possess what's ours. Everyone would like to hear from God that it's harvest time, but don't forget what comes before harvest: seedtime. God will lead you in your sowing, as well. He'll show you what, when, how much, and where to give.

When it comes to sowing, many kick against the leadings of God. They hear from Him and begin to reason, saying, *I don't know what that voice was. I don't think it was God.* If it wasn't God, who was it? Do you really think the devil is leading you to sow into a ministry? If we refuse to respond to God when it's time to sow, there won't be a time to reap. What's more, if we reason away His leadings at seedtime, we won't be able to clearly hear His voice in harvest.

> *For if you live according to the flesh you will die, but if by the Spirit you put to death the deeds of the body, you will live.*
>
> Romans 8:13

What a strong message this verse sends. Living according to the flesh is the opposite of being led by the Spirit. Let's read the first part of this verse this way: *Living according to the flesh will kill your prosperity.*

The carnal, flesh-ruled Christian who lives spiritually empty is not in position to hear from God. That person needs to learn to live full of the Word and the Spirit, experiencing the flow of God's power and life. Much of God's greatest prosperity – feeding a multitude with just a few fish; paying taxes for two people with just one fish – is in the flow of the miraculous. The carnal individual has little idea how to cooperate with God in the flow of the miraculous, and will be excluded until he or she develops spiritually.

Carnality is no friend to the Christian; it is a prosperity killer. We must leave behind carnality, instead developing proficiency in following the leadings of the Spirit. The Spirit-led person will experience success after success.

Chapter 24

DISOBEDIENCE

And all these blessings shall come upon you and overtake you, **if you obey** *the voice of the Lord your God.*

Deuteronomy 28:2

There are many verses in the Bible where the operative word is *if*. This is one such verse. We must clearly understand that, although the love of God is unconditional, the promises and blessings of God are conditional. God will give us His best *if*. . . . This word *if* represents our part of the equation, our side of the deal, our responsibility. We must do our part, He must do His part.

God simply cannot bless us on a whim. He needs a legal right to do for us what He desires. Many would argue, *God can do whatever He pleases, whenever He wants.* Not so. If the Bible is true (which it is), God cannot just do what He wants, when He wants. He is indeed omnipotent, but omnipotence does not dismiss God from the spiritual laws to which He has bound Himself.

When I owned an apartment complex, I had a master key that would unlock any apartment in the building. However, when those units were rented, I could only enter with the tenant's permission. My master key made me all-powerful in the complex, yet I had no legal right to use my power apart from the tenant.

That's exactly how it works with God. He has all power but needs us to give Him the legal right to use it. Look at the following passage:

> *And I heard a loud voice in heaven, saying, Now the salvation and the power and the kingdom of our God and the authority of his Christ have come, for **the accuser of our brothers** has been thrown down, who accuses them day and night before our God. And they have conquered him by the blood of the Lamb and by the word of their testimony, for they loved not their lives even unto death.*
>
> *Revelation 12:10-11*

A LEGAL BASIS

Notice that Satan is called the accuser. He is one unhappy dude, having been stripped of everything that God had ever given him. God passed judgment on him for his actions, kicked him out of Heaven, and sentenced him to a future of torment in Hell. Satan lost his place of authority in Heaven because he disqualified himself from that place. Were he to see God bless someone on Earth who does not qualify for those blessings, Satan would speak up, accuse that person before God, and call God unjust for blessing them.

Since God is just, everything that He does is righteous. He never perverts justice, never twists the law. He does everything legally. Were Satan able to find even one instance where God unjustly blessed someone, he would have the right to demand that his own sentence be overturned and his banishment from Heaven revoked. We must remain in compliance with the laws of the Kingdom in order for God to have the legal right to bless us.

This doesn't mean we must live a sinless life. It's Christ's righteousness by which we live victoriously here on Earth, not our own. It's His blood by which we are cleansed from all sin (1 John 1:7). Jesus has already set us up for every success we could need, however, we must still do our part by living in agreement with what He has done. Look again at verse 12:

They have conquered him by the blood of the Lamb and by the word of their testimony.

How do we overcome the accuser? By agreeing with what God did on our behalf. He sent Jesus to shed His blood, paying the price for our redemption from sin, sickness, and poverty. That's what God did. What's our part? Agree with it. Speak in line with it. God's part was the blood of the Lamb. Our part is the word of our testimony.

Think for a moment about this scenario: a person is arrested, falsely accused of murder. His attorney, a criminal defense expert, knows that his client is innocent, but still must prepare the case for trial. The prosecuting attorney believes this man is guilty and will try to prove it. The attorney gets the accused ready for trial by coaching him how to answer when he takes the witness stand. The attorney tells him, *Only say this.* When the trial begins, the prosecuting attorney lets the accusations rip. He so confuses and pressures the defendant, that the man cries out, *I'm guilty. I did it!*

The defense attorney had a convincing argument prepared, but the defendant's admission of guilt closes the case. He's guilty by admission, by his own testimony. Had the accused spoken what his attorney had told him to say, his attorney could have won the case, and he would have walked free.

This is a picture of how things work in the spirit realm. The accuser, Satan, looks for any excuse to disqualify us before God. He knows that Christ's blood has been shed on our behalf, and that we are really innocent, but if he can get us to admit guilt and let go of our faith, he can still defeat us. Without the right words, Jesus, our high-priest and defense attorney, cannot point to His blood and declare us innocent. We must speak and act in line with what God has done for us. That's what we mean when we speak of *qualifying* or *disqualifying*.

This is the essence of obedience for the Christian. We must do what God has told us to do and say what He has told us to say. Only then is God legally able to bless and increase us. When we disobey, it's the same as when the innocent man admits guilt. No one could help him. If we go against God – disobeying His Word or the leadings of His Spirit – God has no grounds by which to bless us. He must leave us as we are.

OBEDIENCE AND LOVE

Obedience and disobedience are legal issues. They're also love issues. (There's always a legal side and a love side to the things of God.) He does what He does on legal grounds *and* because He loves us. Our obedience ought to be out of love, in response to

His love.

Think about how things work with our children. When our kids comply with our standards and instructions, a door is opened through which we can appropriately reward them. When they fail to comply, we are wrong to reward them and must refrain. Our reward to our children is not something we give them just because they qualify, it's something we give because we love them. Love is the motivation; obedience is the justification.

God cannot reward disobedience. It's wrong from both the love standpoint and from a legal standpoint. Disobedience therefore, is a prosperity killer. We must obey, so the Lord can bring all the blessing He desires into our life.

Believers don't always like hearing about obedience, because they feel as though God is mad at them for the times they may have missed it. No, friends, the opposite is true. He loves you and so desires your success that He has poured out all that He has on your behalf. He just can't get His blessing to you unless you obey. Obedience isn't difficult, but it is necessary. We don't ask things of our children that are beyond their capacity, we just need them to do what we say. Likewise, God needs us to do and say what He says.

> *For this is the love of God, that we keep his commandments. And his commandments are not burdensome.*
>
> *1 John 5:3*

When a person is not a doer of the Word, they are in disobedience. If they refuse to sow, tithe, or repent of sin, they are disobeying. Not walking in love is walking in disobedience. Not living right will disqualify the believer from prosperity. It's not enough to have been given a place of righteousness, we must also obey, displaying the fruits of righteousness (Philippians 1:11).

MUCH TREASURE

In the house of the righteous there is much treasure, but trouble befalls the income of the wicked.

Proverbs 15:6

Disobedience is akin to wickedness, which puts us out of reach of the blessings of God. By contrast, the righteous – the obedient – enjoys much treasure in their house. I like the idea of having much treasure in my house. Not long ago I moved into a house that was bigger and very different from my previous home. Much of the furniture that we had didn't work in the new house and some of the rooms didn't yet have furniture. I know first hand how much it costs to fill a house with fine furniture and decor. Obedience, however, is all that is needed to get the job done.

GOD'S BEST

If you are willing and obedient, you shall eat the good of the land.

Isaiah 1:19

Again we see how the prosperity and promises of God are conditional: God doing His part and we doing ours. This verse, an amazing promise, neatly sums up the entire doctrine of Bible prosperity: *have the right heart, do the right thing, and enjoy God's best.* That's it, folks. It's not very difficult, yet many disqualify somewhere in that simple equation.

Some do the right thing, qualifying through obedience, but don't bring a right heart. We identified a large, open, generous heart as the kind that God can bless. Others have a good heart, but fail to follow through with action. Good intentions alone won't cut it. Both the heart and actions together must come into alignment with God's directions and purpose.

Notice that God wants us to eat the *good of the land.* This is so precious. The *New American Standard Bible* translates this phrase as *the best of the land.* Not just the best in Heaven, but the best here in this land, wherever you live. He wants us to have the best. Jesus died so we could have the best. God is pleased when we have the best. Say it several times: *God wants me to have the best.*

He wants us to eat the best. I don't know if you realize it, but fast food is usually not the best food. (Some people think it is because it's fast, greasy, and cheap.) Premium food costs a lot more than what's on the dollar menu at the drive-thru. See yourself eating better. God doesn't specifically define what *the good* or *the best* is, because, as with other things, it's relative. For some people in some places, any hot, nutritious meal is *the best.*

HIGH-DOLLAR EATING

When I traveled with Brother Hagin, we were in a certain

city ministering, and some of the people from the church were showing us around town. They were pointing out some of the restaurants near our hotel so we would know what was around. As they drove past a certain national chain restaurant, they said, *Now that's your high-dollar eating right there.* I didn't say anything, but in my town, I won't even eat there. In my town, it's low class. In this town, however, it was the best of the land.

We are to believe for God's best, qualifying through obedience. However, we are not to be snobs in this (or any other) area. Jesus didn't just speak of eating the best, He also spoke of eating what is set before you (Luke. 10:8). Someone else's version of the best may be quite different than yours.

Many years ago, I was on a ministry tour in the Philippines with an internationally known gospel artist. This singer was so popular in that country that his music was played over the loud-speakers in the public shopping mall. The day we arrived, our group was honored at a dinner with several heads of state. We were seated on a platform and were served a dinner featuring their finest delicacy: ox tongue. That's not my *best of the land* meal, but because it was their best of the land, I made it mine. No, I didn't eat it all, but I took a few bites and played with the rest so it looked like I was really enjoying it.

If God wants you to eat the best, wouldn't He also want you to wear the best? Sure He would. He's already told us that the flowers of the field are dressed better than King Solomon, and that He would *much more* clothe us (Matthew 6:30). There's a supply for you and me to have the best if we're willing and obedient.

One person's best might be nice overalls. Another person's best might be a nice suit. Whatever your personal situation requires, and whatever your heart desires, you can have the best.

If you're eating well and looking good, what would God want you to drive? The best. Again, that means different things for different people, at different stages of life. For the new mother of triplets, the best might be a nice new van to get her family around. High-end sports cars may fit other people's definition of *the best of the land,* but one of those would be useless to that new mother. Whatever you drive, be faithful with it and keep it clean, so you can qualify for even better at the right time.

If you're driving the best, where would God want you to live? In the best. Stop making excuses for your situation. Stop talking about what you can't have because you are serving God and start talking about what you can have because you are serving God. I know of some people who attend a certain church and travel to the mission field. They are always talking about what they can't have because they're missionaries. Another missionary family in the same church got a new house and these people got mad at them for having it. People need to learn that it's not their calling that keeps them from having the best, it's their doubt and unbelief. You can live in the best at every level.

God has provided the best for us throughout our lives. Our first apartment was in the best complex in town. Our first house was not large, but was the nicest in the neighborhood. Every home we have owned has been a standout home in the neighborhood. We live in the best. I won't have it any other way. If, like our current home, it's not the best when we purchase it, it will be by the time we're done with it. You can have the best in every area of life, as long as you qualify by being willing and obedient.

We must obey God, doing what He's told us to do and going where He's told us to go. You can't disobey and prosper. If God deals with you to give a certain offering and you pretend you didn't hear anything, that's fine. Just know, your disobedience is killing your prosperity. You can spend all day confessing, *My God shall supply all my needs,* but He won't. He can't, because He needs your obedience. What people don't realize is, God often responds to our confession of supply by bringing us an opportunity to sow. He may have a miracle harvest for someone, but it's on the other side of the seed they chose not to sow.

If we'll obey, He'll pay. It sounds so easy because it is, but so many people get derailed in the obedience. We do not get to pick and choose how God will supply for us any more than we get to choose how He will heal us. If God says, *Go wash in the pool of Siloam,* you can't just go wash in the sink and get results. If He says, *Go dip seven times in the Jordan,* you can't just dip twice and get results. We must do His will, His way.

OBEDIENCE AND MIRACLES

In the passage below, some very specific obedience was required, but miraculous results were received. It's the story of the Prophet Elijah and the widow of Zarephath. We noted in an earlier chapter how the prophet had to obey and travel to a place called *there.* Now we see the obedience that was required of the widow, and the prosperity that followed.

> *Then the word of the Lord came to him, "Arise, go to Zare-phath, which belongs to Sidon, and dwell there. Behold, I have commanded a widow there to feed you." So he arose and went to Zarephath. And when he came to the gate of the city, behold, a widow was there gathering sticks. And he called to her and said, "Bring me a little water in a vessel, that I may drink." And as she was going to bring it, he called to her and said, "Bring me a morsel of bread in your hand." And she said, "As the Lord your God lives, I have nothing baked, only a handful of flour in a jar and a little oil in a jug. And now I am gathering a couple of sticks that I may go in and prepare it for myself and my son, that we may eat it and die." And Elijah said to her, "Do not fear; go and do as you have said.* **But first make me a little cake of it and bring it to me, and afterward make something for yourself and your son**. *For thus says the Lord, the God of Israel, 'The jar of flour shall not be spent, and the jug of oil shall not be empty, until the day that the Lord sends rain upon the earth.'" And she went and did as Elijah said. And she and he and her household ate for many days. The jar of flour was not spent, neither did the jug of oil become empty, according to the word of the Lord that he spoke by Elijah.*
>
> *1 Kings 17:8-16*

Wow! What a scene. People get excited about the *thus says the Lord* part of miracles, but we see here that the prophetic promise followed the command of obedience. This woman had to use the last of her resources to bake a cake and serve it to the prophet before making anything for herself and her son. When she obeyed,

God paid, sustaining them throughout the drought. Notice one of the last parts of this passage:

And she went and did as Elijah said. And she and he and her household ate for many days.

She did as Elijah said. What had he said? *Make me a cake first.* It's not unreasonable to believe that, every day, she took care of the man of God first, feeding him before feeding herself and her child. As she obeyed, the miracle continued. This went on for *many days.* This drought lasted for three and a half years. It's reasonable to believe that this miracle of provision – the oil and flour replenishing daily – occurred perpetually for the majority of that time. That's amazing prosperity, but it wasn't just God that did it. The widow had to choose to obey.

Instead of her and her son dying, they remained well fed throughout the famine. Obedience pays richly. The widow, however, couldn't choose to change the prophet's instructions and still call it obedience. She couldn't decide, *Okay, I'll do it, but I'll feed my son first.* Everything in the natural would have dictated that order. Even the prophet likely wouldn't have minded waiting until she and her son had eaten, but God's power only flows His way. Her faith and obedience prepared a place for God's power.

Let's learn from this story. Don't modify God's instructions and call it obedience. He calls some people to move from their hometown to go to a Bible School to prepare for ministry. The family might sense that call with clarity, but the thought of leaving other family and friends is too much for them. Instead of moving, they send a nice check to the Bible School and pretend as though they obeyed God. That doesn't work. God can't be bought. We can't modify God's instructions and be considered obedient.

OBEDIENCE AND REBELLION

The following is the premier passage in the Bible showing God's attitude toward disobedience. In this story, the newly crowned King of Israel, Saul, is commanded to utterly destroy Israel's enemies. The prophet Samuel, who had delivered God's command, was clear that everything: man, woman, child, animal, possessions, etc. was to be destroyed. Saul prevailed against his enemies, yet kept some of the people alive, spared the king, and allowed the people to help themselves to the plunder. The scriptures show the Prophet Samuel confronting Saul about his disobedience, pronouncing judgement upon him on behalf of the Lord.

Why then did you not obey the voice of the Lord? Why did you pounce on the spoil and do what was evil in the sight of the Lord?" And Saul said to Samuel, "I have obeyed the voice of the Lord. I have gone on the mission on which the Lord sent me. I have brought Agag the king of Amalek, and I have devoted the Amalekites to destruction. But the people took of the spoil, sheep and oxen, the best of the things devoted to destruction, to sacrifice to the Lord your God in Gilgal." And Samuel said, "Has the Lord as great delight in burnt offerings and sacrifices, as in obeying the voice of the Lord? Behold, **to obey is better than sacrifice,** *and to listen than the fat of rams. For rebellion is as the sin of divination, and presumption is as iniquity and idolatry. Because you have rejected the word of the Lord, he has also rejected you from being king."*

1 Samuel 15:19-23

Saul made every excuse he could think of to justify his behavior. He lied and blamed the people, basically saying, *This was all just a big misunderstanding.* No, it was plain old disobedience, the same kind that got Adam and Eve kicked out of the garden. Saul thought that he was okay because he had indeed obeyed some of what God had told him to do. He soon learned that, with God, partial obedience is the same as total disobedience.

Saul told Samuel, *We saved these sheep to sacrifice to God.* God responded, saying that He would rather have obedience than offerings. He's exactly the same today. You can't buy your way into His favor and power, but you can access those things through obedience. Let's bring full obedience to our Father, understanding that disobedience is a prosperity killer. If we will be willing and obedient, the best of the land will be ours.

Chapter 25

DISHONOR

I minister often on the subject of honor. The reason I emphasize that subject is because God has emphasized it to me. He showed me long ago how honor could help my life. A simple definition of honor is *assigning the proper weight or value to a person or thing*. It has to do with seeing things the way God sees them and acting accordingly. Honor is a major issue where finances and material possessions are concerned.

*"Honor your father and mother" (this is the first commandment with a promise), "**that it may go well with you** and that you may live long in the land."*

Ephesians 6:2-3

When we introduced the subject of prosperity in the first chapter of this book, we pointed out that one definition is simply to have things go well. That's what Paul was saying here. John brings out the same thought in his writing:

*Beloved, I pray that **all may go well with you** and that you may he in good health, as it goes well with your soul.*

3 John 1:2

In our text in Ephesians 6, Paul connects honor to prosperity and long life. Honoring our parents is certainly an important way to show honor, yet it's not the only way that honor is expressed. Honor is to be present in every area of our lives. We could simplify Ephesians 6:2-3 by reading it this way: *If we will honor, we will prosper.*

RUTH

One of the best examples of the connection between honor and prosperity is found in the Old Testament story of Ruth. If you are serious about prosperity (I imagine you are if you've read this far), I would recommend taking time now to read the four short chapters of the book of Ruth. I will highlight just one verse here:

> *But Ruth said, "Do not urge me to leave you or to return from following you. For where you go I will go, and where you lodge I will lodge. Your people shall be my people, and your God my God.*
>
> Ruth 1:16

Here's what happened: Ruth was a Moabite girl who married into an Israelite family that had been living in her nation. In the process of time, Ruth's husband, father-in-law, and brother-in-law all died. All the men of the family were now gone, which, in that day, meant all the wage earners in the family were gone. Having married into a family in covenant with God, Ruth recognized that these people lived differently from the people in her nation. They knew the Lord.

Ruth's mother-in-law, Naomi, had obviously been a blessing

to her daughters-in-law because neither wanted to leave her after the men died. Naomi, understandably concerned about supporting the girls, tried to send them back to their homes. One daughter-in-law finally did leave. Ruth, however, refused to leave. It wasn't that she wanted to mooch off of Naomi, rather, she sensed an obligation to help see after her. And, there was no way she was going to leave the living God to go back to the false gods her people worshipped.

Ruth's show of loyalty to Naomi was a major show of honor. When they returned to Naomi's hometown, Ruth immediately tried to find work to support the two of them. She was determined to take care of Naomi the way Naomi had taken care of her. How did God respond to Ruth's show of honor? He brought the richest, most honorable man in town to be her husband. Ruth and Naomi were taken care of for life. Remember, Ruth was an outsider (not an Israelite) but honor will bring anyone into God's inner circle. Ruth and her husband, Boaz, served God, had a child named Jesse, and later a grandchild named David, the greatest king that Israel has ever known.

WHERE'S MY HONOR?

"A son honors his father, and a servant his master. If then I am a father, where is my honor? And if I am a master, where is my fear? says the Lord of hosts to you, O priests, who despise my name. But you say, 'How have we despised your name?' By offering polluted food upon my altar. But you say, 'How have we polluted you?' By saying that the Lord's table may be despised. When you offer blind animals in sacrifice, is that

not evil? And when you offer those that are lame or sick, is that not evil? Present that to your governor; will he accept you or show you favor? says the Lord of hosts. And now entreat the favor of God, that he may be gracious to us. With such a gift from your hand, will he show favor to any of you? says the Lord of hosts. Oh that there were one among you who would shut the doors, that you might not kindle fire on my altar in vain! I have no pleasure in you, says the Lord of hosts, and I will not accept an offering from your hand.

Malachi 1:6-10

This passage in Malachi was a rebuke to the priests of Israel. Because every believer today is a priest unto God (1 Peter 2:5), there are principles in this passage that apply to us. One of the main jobs of the Old Testament priest was to offer sacrifices. Today's priests (believers) also bring offerings before the Lord. God's issue with these Israelite priests was not that they were failing to offer the required sacrifices, but that they were offering them in the wrong way and with a wrong heart. Listen to these strong words from the Lord in verse 6:

If then I am a father, where is my honor?

Should our Father, who has given everything for us, ever have to ask for honor? Never. He should never have to tell us to reorder our priorities or put Him first. It's our job to maintain a heart of honor, keeping these things in order.

What was the big issue? They were devaluing God by the offerings they were bringing. They offered polluted food on the altar. They offered blind, deformed, and sick animals as a sacrifice.

Their offerings were in no way a reflection of the greatness of God. Let's talk for a moment about how these kinds of offerings would look if offered to a man instead of to God.

Let's say you were bringing an offering to your pastor. Can you imagine knocking on his door with a grocery bag in hand saying, *Pastor I have this milk that has gone sour, some moldy cheese, a loaf of stale bread, and some putrid meat. I was going to throw these things out, but then I thought, 'Hey, why not bring them to you for you and your family to eat?'*

This scenario, unfortunately, is not unlike what happens in some churches. Instead of paying to dump their old furniture, people drop it off at the pastor's house as an offering. Then they want a tax receipt for leaving their garbage on his porch. If you are having trouble deciding between throwing something out and giving it to your pastor, let me help you decide: throw it out.

Hopefully, none of us would ever do this to our pastor. That kind of offering says, *Pastor, you are unimportant and of little value. I'll give you things I wouldn't give to anyone I really cared about.* When people give God their garbage, or an amount of money that is disproportionate to the place He is to have in our lives, they are saying the same thing to Him. They are saying, in essence, *God, I really don't care about you.*

When these priests were bringing God their crippled animals, it grieved Him. Why? Because, in the marketplace, those animals have no value. They are worthless. When you give something of no value to someone, it says something about their value in your life. How would a wife feel if her husband brought her home a gift that he found in the garbage? How does God feel when we give Him (or His representatives, like our pastor) our leftovers and garbage? We know exactly how He feels. He told us. You can't treat the Lord like trash and expect to walk in His best. As we saw in the story of Ruth, God honors those that honor him (see 1 Samuel 2:30).

HONOR AND THE TITHE

This passage in Malachi 1 is not the end of the Lord's rebuke. He goes on to talk about treating one's spouse with honor. Then, in Malachi 3, the Lord again speaks of offerings. How we handle our money is one of the biggest indicators of honor there is.

> *Will man rob God? Yet you are robbing me. But you say, 'How have we robbed you?' In your tithes and contributions. You are cursed with a curse, for you are robbing me, the whole nation of you. Bring the full tithe into the storehouse, that there may be food in my house. And thereby put me to the test, says the Lord of hosts, if I will not open the windows of heaven for you and pour down for you a blessing until there is no more need. I will rebuke the devourer for you, so that it will not destroy the fruits of your soil, and your vine in the field shall not fail to bear, says the Lord of hosts. Then all nations will call you blessed, for you will be a land of delight, says the Lord of hosts.*
>
> *Malachi 3:8-12*

This passage is still speaking of honor. God is saying that He wants to bless His people abundantly: a level of blessing that can't be contained. He wants His people free from the domain of the enemy. He wants us fruitful and productive. He has made provision for all of these things to occur, but none of them can happen if honor is not in place. Honor, and honor's actions, are necessary if we are to experience God's full prosperity. When honor is missing, so is prosperity. Dishonor is a prosperity killer.

Many in our day do not care for this passage in Malachi. They talk about how tithing is part of the law and has been done away with. That position is not exactly correct, but my question is this: has honor been done away with? Has taking care of God's house passed by the wayside? Of course not. The believer is still required to place the highest possible value on God, His house, His people, and His things. If that doesn't at least equal the tithe (a tenth) of your income, your level of honor is not high enough.

HONOR AND FIRSTFRUITS

Honor the Lord with your wealth and with the firstfruits of all your produce; then your barns will be filled with plenty, and your vats will be bursting with wine.

Proverbs 3:9-10

This is another passage that often trips people up, for it contains the word *firstfruits*. Some say that we should give special firstfruits offerings that are in addition to our tithe. Others say that, in our day, all that's required are tithes and offerings. Still others say that we should just be led and do what seems right. There is truth to each of these statements, yet there are problems with each.

In the New Covenant, we are not to do *anything* in a ritualistic or legalistic fashion. We need not conform to every detail of Moses' law, for we are no longer under that law. (Even the people who were under the law were not supposed to keep it in a ritualistic or legalistic manner. They were to perform the law from their heart.) However, when things that were regulated by the law (such as tithing or firstfruits offerings) are also expressions of the law of honor, it's appropriate to continue practicing them. Honor is always appropriate.

The concept of firstfruits means that when something new comes into your life, perhaps a new income stream, you take the first part of it and give it to the Lord. In an agricultural society, the first crops to come up would belong to the Lord. The firstborn of one's livestock would be the Lord's. In our business-driven society, the first payment from a new source of income would be the Lord's.

I don't discourage people from giving such offerings because the whole premise is based on honor. A person is saying, *Lord, I recognize that you brought this increase into my life, so I am giving you the first instance of it.* There's nothing wrong with that. Any opportunity to show honor is an opportunity we should take. I have practiced this very thing as new income streams have opened to me. When I began my current phase of ministry, I took the first offering that came in and sowed it to my local church. We don't require or force people do this (just like we don't force any offering), but there is scriptural precedent for it, and it's an honorable thing to do.

BURSTING OUT

If you still don't like the word *firstfruits*, are you okay with the word *first*? That's really the emphasis in this passage: putting God first. This verse starts out with the word *honor*. We honor God best when we put Him first. Notice in verse 10, that a great promise is attached to putting God first:

Then your barns will be filled with plenty, and your vats will be bursting with wine.

I like that. Especially the part about our vats bursting. When something is bursting (or, as some would say, *busting*), it means that there was more than could be contained. That's what Malachi chapter three was talking about when it spoke of God pouring out an overflowing blessing. I want to get into that bursting level of blessing. Honor causes our level of blessing to exceed our capacity. Honor makes things burst out.

Do you want your business to burst out? Do you want your ministry to burst out? Do you want your career to burst out? It only happens for the believer who puts God first. Notice that the passage specified a certain order: we put God first, *then* our barns get filled. We must maintain this order. It's God first, *then* us, not the other way around.

Say it several times: *First God, then me.*

Most believers do not bring honor to God by putting Him first. Instead of bursting out, many go belly up. When there's an absence of honor, the barns don't get filled and the presses don't burst out. Let's get to that bursting level of blessing by bringing honor to God, putting Him first.

Chapter 26

THE SUM OF THE MATTER

We have exposed many of the prosperity killers that can hold a person back from receiving God's best. True prosperity is the plan of God for every believer and is readily available, but it only works one way: His way. When we try to modify or alter His plans, achieving prosperity some other way, it just doesn't work. Money alone is not prosperity. True prosperity always includes God.

We have seen how the scriptures address every side of this mountain of truth. Prosperity can involve money and great possessions, which some are not in position to handle. This subject is both holy and deadly. In order to help keep us on the right side of the truth, the scriptures contain over two thousand references to money.

There are two passages from the ministry of Jesus that, together, form a well-rounded picture of the doctrine of prosperity. They show the heart of God, reveal the heart of a true believer, and place extreme prosperity in its proper place. If a person desires to view, in snapshot form, God's position on the subject of prosperity, these passages are a great place to start.

On one occasion, while the crowd was pressing in on him to hear the word of God, he was standing by the lake of Gennesaret, and he saw two boats by the lake, but the fishermen had gone out of them and were washing their nets. Getting into one of the boats, which was Simon's, he asked him to put out a little from the land. And he sat down and taught the people from the boat. And when he had finished speaking, he said to Simon, "Put out into the deep and let down your nets for a catch." And Simon answered, "Master, we toiled all night and took nothing! But at your word I will let down the nets." And when they had done this, they enclosed a large number of fish, and their nets were breaking. They signaled to their partners in the other boat to come and help them. And they came and filled both the boats, so that they began to sink.

Luke 5:1-8

After this Jesus revealed himself again to the disciples by the Sea of Tiberias, and he revealed himself in this way. Simon Peter, Thomas (called the Twin), Nathanael of Cana in Galilee, the sons of Zebedee, and two others of his disciples were together. Simon Peter said to them, "I am going fishing." They said to him, "We will go with you." They went out and got into the boat, but that night they caught nothing. Just as day was breaking, Jesus stood on the shore; yet the disciples did not know that it was Jesus. Jesus said to them, "Children, do you have any fish?" They answered him, "No." He said to them, "Cast the net on the right side of the boat, and you will find some." So they cast it, and now they were not able to haul it in, because of the quantity of fish. That disciple whom Jesus loved therefore said to Peter, "It is the Lord!" When Simon Peter heard that it was the Lord, he put on his outer garment, for he was stripped for work, and threw himself into the sea. The other disciples came in the boat, dragging the net full of fish, for they were not far from the land, but about a hundred yards off. When they got out on land, they saw a charcoal fire in place, with fish laid out on it, and bread. Jesus said to them, "Bring some of the fish that you have just caught." So Simon Peter went aboard and hauled the net ashore, full of large fish, 153 of them. And although there were so many, the net was not torn.

John 21:1-11

The first of these passages shows the Lord at the beginning of His earthly ministry, while the second shows Him at the end. He began and ended His ministry by demonstrating miraculous provision. Prosperity was, and is, an identifying characteristic of the ministry of Jesus. It's interesting that some who would later become apostles were introduced to Jesus by experiencing extreme provision. Prosperity haters often comment that provision will never draw a person to Christ. It did here.

Think about this second story. The disciples were taking what looked to be a step backward. Jesus was gone, and they didn't quite know what to do, so they began doing what they knew: fishing. Notice that this passage begins by saying, *Jesus revealed himself.* He revealed Himself by displaying a familiar characteristic, flashing His calling card of miracle provision that they had seen over and over throughout His ministry. When they saw the fish, John immediately recognized who was at work, saying, *It is the Lord.*

Many people in our day see prosperity and say, *That's the devil, it can't be God.* With all due respect, I'm going to agree with what John said: it's the Lord. When we've done all that we know in the natural with no results, and then experience a miracle harvest, it's not the devil, it's God.

These passages show us that laboring in the flesh alone won't get the job done. Prosperity is never just natural; there's always a spiritual element. We need that which only the power of God can bring. It's not enough to have a job, a business, an income stream; we need God's prosperity – His blessing – His increase.

The prosperity of God can be very, very big, because He's so big. People understandably get concerned if a huge dog begins playing with a tiny baby; that dog could crush the child without meaning to. In the same way, God's deposits of increase can be hard on our equipment. We might need to mend our nets, bail water from the boat, or mop up the overflow when He's done. So be it. That's just who He is. In both of these cases, the increase that came was dangerously close to exceeding the recipient's capacity to receive. We must enlarge our hearts and minds to be able to handle more of His infinite blessing.

Finally, notice verse 11 in Luke chapter 5:

And when they had brought their boats to land, they left everything and followed him.

In both of these accounts, the followers of Jesus experienced overwhelming provision. And, in both cases, that provision didn't turn them away from God, it turned them toward God. It's not the stuff that we love, it's God whom we love. It's not the gift that we're obsessed with, it's the giver. Those 153 large fish were 153 more than they had caught after a full night's work, but Peter jumped right into the water, swimming away from the fish and toward the Master. May we possess the same quality of heart and clarity of sight.

God is a ship-sinking, net-breaking, cup-running-over, more-cattle-than-the-land-can-hold, overflowing, more-than-you-can-contain God. He wants to make you an example of His goodness. He wants to do things for you that will make your friends and neighbors ask how it happened. He wants you blessed. He is looking for ways to show His love to you. Let Him be as big as He is, to you.

Your mission? Stay away from the prosperity killers.

SALVATION

The most important decision you can make in life is the decision to receive Jesus Christ as your personal Lord and Savior. It is a decision to turn from sin and self, and to follow God, every day and in every way.

This decision to receive Christ is what the Bible calls being *born-again*, or being *saved*. Without this salvation experience, people are doomed to failure in life and eternity in hell. Success and eternal life belong to the believer in Christ. If you have been reading this book and don't know that you have been born-again, it's time to make the decision to follow Christ.

Read what God says in His word about this great experience:

Truly, truly, I say to you, whoever hears my word and believes him who sent me has eternal life. He does not come into judgment, but has passed from death to life.

John 5:24

For God so loved the world, that he gave his only Son, that whoever believes in him should not perish but have eternal life. For God did not send his Son into the world to condemn the world, but in order that the world might be saved through him.

John 3:16-17

For by grace you have been saved through faith. And this is not your own doing; it is the gift of God, not a result of works, so that no one may boast.

Ephesians 2:8-9

If you confess with your mouth that Jesus is Lord and believe in your heart that God raised him from the dead, you will be saved. For with the heart one believes and is justified, and with the mouth one confesses and is saved.

Romans 10:9-10

Because our sin has separated us from God, we need a savior, one who would take our place in eternal death and give us eternal life. Jesus is that savior; the only one qualified to take our place.

And this is the testimony, that God gave us eternal life, and this life is in his Son. Whoever has the Son has life; whoever does not have the Son of God does not have life.

1 John 5:11-12

Receive Christ right now by praying a prayer such as this one. Speak the words from your heart, and God will hear and answer you.

Dear God, I see that my sins have separated me from You and I repent of sin. Thank You that you loved me so much that You sent Jesus to suffer and die on my behalf, so that I could receive eternal life. I believe Jesus died for me and rose again, and I receive Him as my Savior right now. Jesus, You are my Lord and I'll live for You from this day on. Thank You Father for saving me!

If you prayed that and meant it, be assured that God has done exactly what you asked. You are now His child. You have been born into His family. This verse now describes you, the new creation:

Therefore, if anyone is in Christ, he is a new creation. The old has passed away; behold, the new has come.

2 Corinthians 5:17

There are some additional steps you should take now that you are a follower of Jesus Christ. The most important step is to find a good local church. The pastor there will minister to you and help you grow in the things of God. Make sure your church believes and teaches the Bible and allows the Holy Spirit to work freely. Your pastor can help teach you about other steps to get started in the Christian life, such as studying the Word of God, being filled with the Holy Spirit, tithing, and serving in the local church.

Congratulations on making life's most important decision!

ABOUT THE AUTHOR

Faith in God's Word, and constant reliance on the Holy Spirit have been the keys to success in the life and ministry of Rev. Joel Siegel. Raised and educated as a Jew, Joel Siegel, at age 18, had a life-transforming encounter with Christ that brought him true purpose and fulfillment.

Rev. Joel Siegel began preaching and teaching the Word of God soon after he was saved in 1986. He entered full-time ministry in 1990, serving for three years as the music director for the acclaimed gospel music group *Truth*. Truth's road schedule took Joel and his wife Amy worldwide to over 300 cities a year, ministering in churches and on college campuses.

From 1993 to 2000, Joel was the musical director for Rev. Kenneth E. Hagin's RHEMA Singers & Band. In addition to assisting Rev. Hagin in his crusade meetings, Joel produced eight music projects for the ministry, including his first solo release, *Trust & Obey*.

From 2000 to 2011, Joel and Amy (herself a skilled pastor and worship leader), served as the founding pastors of Good News Family Church in Orchard Park, NY. During this time, they were frequently asked to host shows for the TCT Christian Television Network. Joel regularly hosted their popular *Ask The Pastor* program.

Rev. Joel Siegel spends his time ministering to congregations in the U.S. and abroad, passionately endeavoring to fulfill his assignment to help lead this generation into the move of God that will usher in the return of Christ.

The Siegels make their home in Colorado. Joel oversees Faith Church Colorado in the town of Castle Rock, where Amy is lead pastor.

For music recordings, audio teaching series, books, and other resources, or to invite Rev. Joel Siegel to minister at a church or event, please visit www.joelsiegel.org.